Christmas Gifts from the Chanukah Crowd:

The Extraordinary Contributions of American Jews to Christmas

By Denise Noe

BearManor Media

Orlando, Florida

Christmas Gifts for the Chanukah Crowd:
The Extraordinary Contributions of American Jews to Christmas
© 2021 Denise Noe. All Rights Reserved.

No portion of this publication may be reproduced, stored, and/or copied electronically (except for academic use as a source), nor transmitted in any form or by any means without the prior written permission of the publisher and/or author.

Published in the USA by
BearManor Media
1317 Edgewater Dr. #110
Orlando, FL 32804
www.BearManorMedia.com

Softcover Edition
ISBN: 978-1-62933-647-3

Printed in the United States of America

Table of Contents

Preface   ix

1) Christmas in the World, Christmas in America   1

2) A War on Christmas ... by Jews?   11

3) Major Christmas Songs Written and/or Composed by Jews   25

4) A Potpourri of Christmas Films with Strong Jewish Input   69

5) The Holiday Called Chanukah   133

6) Kwanzaa, Yule/Solstice, and Other Special December Days   143

7) Happy Holidays ... to Everyone!   163

Bibliography   165

Index   175

This Gentile writer dedicates this book to her late Jewish best friend, Jeffrey Venitt.

Preface

Each December in modern America, the radio waves fill with Christmas songs while television sets and movie theaters feature Christmas-themed motion pictures. Homes and businesses boast Christmas trees typically hung with tinsel and brightly colored balls, the trees frequently topped by little angel figurines. Gifts wrapped in special Christmas-themed paper lie around the base of these ubiquitous Christmas trees. Shoppers throng into stores during the "Christmas Rush" in search of Christmas cards and presents.

In the United States, Christmas has been a federal holiday since 1870. (A federal holiday has been designated as such by the U.S. Congress. On a federal holiday, non-essential government offices are closed and federal employees taking that day off receive the same pay as if they had worked. If such a holiday falls on a weekend, it is often observed as a federal holiday on a weekday.) Most American schoolchildren and working people enjoy a treasured Christmas vacation that often starts several days, or even a week or more, prior to Christmas Day and may last through New Year's.

However, for the last several decades, December has also become a time at which some commentators loudly lament an alleged "War on Christmas." The celebration of this holiday is said to be under siege from forces trying to depreciate Christmas or downplay it and perhaps even eliminate this day as a special day. According to such observers, these anti-Christmas forces would like Christmas to disappear but, unable to immediately outlaw the celebration of a holiday that is dear to so many people, they weasel their way toward that end by ripping away as much public evidence of it as possible. They use the courts to remove symbols of Christmas from public places. Another tactic said to reflect anti-Christmas sentiment is the practice of encouraging government agencies, private business, and individuals to substitute "holiday" for "Christmas" as in "Happy Holidays" instead of "Merry Christmas" and "Holiday Season" rather than "Christmas Season."

Various villains are fingered as threats to Christmas. Liberals and secularists are usually said to be the culprits trying to rob the rest of us of this cherished holiday. There are also people who say that Jews are attacking Christmas.

The idea that Jews are real-life Grinches stealing Christmas from their Gentile neighbors is undercut by the interesting irony that many of the most popular Christmas songs were written and/or composed by Jews. Additionally, Jews have also contributed mightily to Christmas-themed motion pictures. Indeed, an astonishing amount of contemporary Christmas celebration originated with Jewish people.

And therein hangs a tale — one rich in tragedy and humor, at once heartbreaking and heartwarming, tragic and triumphant. The story of American Jewry's contributions to Christmas is a story about what it means to be Jewish, what it means to be Christian, and what it means to be American. It is a story about tolerance and intolerance, persecution and perseverance, difference and sameness. Ultimately, it is a fascinating, complex, and deeply meaningful story about what it means to be human – and to live in a world in which different people must live with their differences.

Many things in this book will be described as products of "Jewish and Gentile collaboration." My life was personally enriched by my friendship with the Jewish man to whom this book is dedicated, Jeffrey Venitt. Our friendship became so close that, without ever agreeing to do it, we talked on the phone each morning. Indeed, my day was not started until I spoke with Jeff. Although we often disagreed, I respected his opinions. We discussed the contributions of Jewish people to Christmas and the possibility of my writing on the subject; he strongly encouraged me to do so. Oddly, *after* becoming intrigued by the contributions of Jews to Christmas, this Gentile made an unexpected discovery. A relative of mine on my mother's side researched the family genealogy and discovered that we have Jewish ancestry. That I have some Jewish ancestry hardly makes me Jewish. The amount of such ancestry is less than one-quarter – the minimum amount that would have put an innocent person of Jewish heritage in a death camp in Nazi Germany. I remain Gentile. But knowing that I have such ancestry is a strong reminder to me of the links between different peoples on this planet. It is indeed a small world.

Chapter 1
Christmas in the World, Christmas in America

Each year, billions of people celebrate Christmas in December, usually on December 25. Most Christians observe Christmas as the birth of their Savior, Jesus Christ, while many non-Christians celebrate it as a cultural holiday. This widely celebrated holiday is observed in varied ways over the world with its celebration marked by a potpourri of activities having origins that are Christian, pre-Christian, religious, and secular/cultural. Some of the most popular Christmastime activities are putting up and decorating Christmas trees, hanging mistletoe, exchanging cards, exchanging gifts, singing and listening to Christmas songs, and watching Christmas-themed movies. People often attend special church services and enact Nativity scenes in which the New Testament story about the birth of Jesus is acted out. There are displays of Nativity scenes showing the birth of the Son of God in a stable, the Virgin Mary and Joseph looking on, often accompanied by the Three Wise Men or by shepherds. There are displays of Santa Claus and the reindeers and elves who are his assistants and associates. Children sit on the knees of department store Santa Clauses who coax the children to reveal what they hope to get as Christmas presents. Families frequently gather together for special dinners that are, in America, apt to feature ham or turkey; in some nations, goose is likely to grace the table for Christmas dinner. Fruitcakes are traditionally often served for dessert.

Although Christmas may well be the most cherished holiday of the majority of modern Christians, and is dear to many non-Christians as well, the earliest Christians did not celebrate the birth of Jesus.

The designation of time periods that run into the thousands of years requires a digression that is itself quite relevant to the main issues examined in this book. There has long been a tradition of fixing the period prior to the last 2,000 some years as "B.C.," which means "Before Christ" and the period of the last 2,000 years "A.D.," meaning "Anno Domini" or "In the Year of Our Lord," referring to the year in which Jesus was believed to have been born and every year following his birth. In recent years, "B.C.E," meaning "Before the Common Era," and "C.E.," meaning "Common Era" are frequently used. This author will use both terms with a slash between them.

For the first three centuries A.D./C.E., Christians placed primary emphasis on the day the faith believes Jesus arose from the dead, and celebrated his resurrection, or what is now called Easter. Britannica.com, reports, "During the first two centuries of Christianity, there was strong opposition to recognizing the births of martyrs or, for that matter, of Jesus." The "birthdays," church authorities argued, were the dates of their martyrdom and, in the case of the Savior, his resurrection.

Another reason the earliest Christians may not have celebrated the anniversary of Jesus' birth is that the New Testament never specifies that date. The Christian narrative as given in the New Testament states that Jesus was born in Bethlehem to the Virgin Mary and her husband Joseph who had to travel there to register for a census. Finding no room at the inn, the couple took refuge in a stable. In that stable, the Virgin Mary gave birth to the baby Jesus. "Wise men from the east" are said to have seen a star in the sky that guided them to find this very special child, bringing "gold, and frankincense, and myrrh" as gifts. An angel appeared to shepherds who told them, "Unto you is born this day in the city of David a Savior, which is Christ the Lord."

The shepherds followed the guidance of the angel and found the stable where Mary and Joseph were with baby Jesus "wrapped in swaddling clothes" lying in a manger.

The account of shepherds attending to the birth has led at least some scholars and others to conclude that Jesus was not born on December 25 but was born at some point in spring when it is more likely shepherds would be out at night with their flocks. That Joseph and Mary were in Bethlehem for a census has also been pointed to as making it unlikely these events took place in December.

However, although "Christmas" did not exist for the earliest Christians, the latter part of winter was celebrated by some people. Indeed, the latter part of winter was a time of celebration for hundreds, even thousands, of years before the Christian religion was founded. A "solstice" is the shortest day of the year and there is one in spring and one in winter. The "winter solstice" usually occurs very close to December 25, on December 21 or 22. People have long put an emphasis on the winter solstice because it means the harshest of the cold weather is past or soon to be past and that better weather, including longer days and more sunlight, is on its way. History.com observes, "The end of December was a perfect time for celebration in most areas of Europe. At that time of year, most cattle were slaughtered so they would not have to be fed during the winters. For many, it was the only time of year when they had a supply of fresh meat. In addition, most wine and beer made during the year was finally fermented and ready for drinking."

Throughout ancient times, Scandinavian or Norse tribes, as well as Germanic tribes, celebrated what they called Yule, a period that started at about December 21 and lasted through the start of January. Since the sunshine was about to return, big logs were brought into the home and burned in the belief that each spark of the fire represented a piglet or a calf that would be born the next year. People would also bring evergreens into the home. Since the evergreen is impervious to the freezing of winter, it was regarded as a perfect symbol of the ability of the world to survive the cold and live again after the worst of winter. During Yule, Norse and Germanic peoples stayed indoors (understandably) where they feasted on their many slaughtered cattle, drank and danced and enjoyed revelry. In the places that are now Germany, the awful weather was not the only reason for remaining indoors as a common belief was that the god Odin flew through the area during the winter nights and would decide who would do well and who would die. Fearful that Odin might look on them negatively, they took refuge inside to enjoy the burning of the logs, the aroma and beauty of the evergreens, and the joys of feasting, drinking, and dancing.

Winter was not as severe in Rome but it was still a hardship. Saturnalia was the title of the main winter Roman celebration and it honored Saturn, the god of agriculture. Saturnalia typically started the week before the winter solstice was expected and lasted about a month's time. Many businesses and schools closed for this period. The celebration was often rowdy and raucous as it included feasting and the free flowing of alcoholic beverages. Romans also had a Saturnalia practice of turning the social tables with slaves and masters playfully trading places. One sub-set of the celebration was Juvenalia, a special feast that honored Rome's children. Finally, December 25 was a date observed by some Romans in a far more sober manner as the birthday of Mithra, commonly called "the God of the Unconquerable Sun." History.com reports, "For some Romans, Mithra's birthday was the most sacred day of the year."

After centuries of not recognizing Jesus' birthday, it began to be celebrated in the fourth century A.D. WhyChristmas.com states, "The first recorded date of Christmas being celebrated on December 25th was in 336, during the time of the Roman Emperor Constantine (he was the first Christian Roman Emperor). But it was not an official Roman state festival at this time." Britannica.com relates, "December 25 was first identified as the date of Jesus' birth by Sextus Julius Africanus in 221 and later became the universally accepted date." Around 350 A.D./C.E. Pope Julius I declared that Jesus was born on December 25. The reasons for this are unclear with some people believing it was chosen because it coincided with the birthdate of Mithra. Perhaps, some speculate, Pope Julius I wanted to transfer the honor the pagans gave to their Sun God to the Son of God. Another possibility is that at least some Christian scholars identified the Spring Equinox as the date of the world's creation, and believed it likely God would make that date the time to conceive Jesus, putting his conception at March 25. Thus, it is likely he would have been born nine months later on December 25. As WhyChristmas.com relates, "A very early Christian tradition said that the day when Mary was told that she would have a very special baby, Jesus (called the Annunciation) was on March 25th — and it's still celebrated today on the 25th [of] March. Nine months after the 25th [of] March is the 25th [of] December." It is also possible that December was favored as the month for Jesus to be born since the founder of the Christian faith was born into Judaism and the Jewish Festival of Lights, which is spelled either Chanukah or Hanukkah in English, takes place in December. WhyChristmas.com elaborates, "Hanukah celebrates when the Jewish people were able to re-dedicate and worship in their Temple, in Jerusalem, again following many years of not being allowed to practice their religion." [A later chapter in this book discusses Chanukah.]

Initially, the name given to the celebration of the date on which Jesus was said to have been born was the Feast of the Nativity. The celebration of the Feast of the Nativity spread through the Christian world and it made its way to Egypt by 432 A.D./C.E., to England by the latter part of the sixth century A.D./C.E., and to Scandinavia by the eighth century A.D./C.E. Britannica.com comments, "Christmas began to be widely celebrated with a specific liturgy in the 9th century." The Feast of the Nativity was often observed with a special Mass of Christ. The term "Mass of Christ" eventually became "Christmas."

By the Middle Ages, Christianity had pretty much displaced paganism. There is a great deal of disagreement among historians about the extent to which pagan practices may have persisted, especially in private, but at least officially, being a Christian was the European norm. Christmas was, appropriately, observed with special attention to church attendance. However, the pagan roots of Winter Solstice and Yule were evident in the festivities that took place outside church doors. Historians compare the booze-besotted and carnival-like Medieval revelries held around December 25 to Mardi Gras.

Christmas was celebrated with the crowning of a "Lord of Misrule" whose subjects were peasants going to the homes of the affluent to demand "gifts" of fine food and strong drink. The upper class people had to humor the followers of the Lord of Misrule or risk their homes being attacked.

Exact beginnings for many Christmas customs are difficult to pinpoint but it is known that Renaissance writer Sebastian Brant recorded in his 1494 work, *The Ship of Fools*, that branches of fir trees were placed in homes during the Christmas season. There are records from 1605 of Christmas fir trees decorated with apples and from 1611 of such trees decorated with candles.

The early seventeenth century saw the rise of Puritanism in England and these religious reformers took a dim view of what had become of Christmas. They regarded Christmas as profoundly un-Christian both because of its alleged pagan roots and because the revelries accompanying it were often decidedly non-holy. By 1645, Oliver Cromwell and his Puritan followers had won the English Civil War and executed the defeated King Charles I. This group of devout Christians waged a genuine war on Christmas with the result that Christmas was outlawed in England. This did not cause the holiday to disappear but to go underground. As noted in the History show "Christmas Unwrapped," "Christmas pie became mince pie but tasted just as delicious."

The desire among much of the populace to bring back Christmas was a factor in the Restoration of the Monarchy that put King Charles II on the throne. After he had the crown on his head, King Charles II repaid his supporters by legalizing Christmas. Christmas customs continued to evolve and, as Britannica.com notes, "Toward the end of the 18th century the practice of giving gifts to family members became well established. Theologically, the day reminded Christians of God's gift of Jesus to humankind even as the coming of the Wise Men, or Magi, to Bethlehem suggested that Christmas was somehow related to giving gifts." The Britannica.com article further notes that the gift giving practice went "back to the 15th century."

In the New World, the Pilgrims who landed at Plymouth Rock were just as committed, if not more so, than their fellows back in England, to ridding their environment of rowdy behavior and practices they viewed as holdovers from paganism. The Pilgrims of Plymouth Rock and its surrounding areas did not observe Christmas and strongly discouraged its observance. In 1659, Christmas was outlawed in the city of Boston and a fine of five shillings, a large amount at that time, imposed on malefactors caught celebrating the banned holiday. Of course, the daring continued observing Christmas in secret. Nevertheless, it would remain illegal in Boston until 1681.

Not all of European heritage who populated the New World lived in anti-Christmas colonies. Captain John Smith said Christmas was celebrated in Jamestown. Indeed, History.com notes, "The first eggnog made in the United States was consumed in Captain John Smith's 1607 Jamestown settlement."

After the United States won independence from Britain, becoming its own country, things English fell into disfavor — and Christmas was among them. The celebration of Christmas did not cease but it was not a publicly accepted and applauded holiday and certainly not one popular with devout Christians.

As the nineteenth century dawned, so did forces that led America to reinvent Christmas. The early 1800s saw the Industrial Revolution in full swing, along with growing and acrimonious class conflict. The wealthy felt threatened not only by the low-paid factory workers they employed but by large groups of the unemployed and unconnected. Thus, the rowdy goings-on typical of Christmastime could lead to outright rioting during the season.

That changed with a changed -- and brightened-- view of Christmas. 1819 saw the publication of *The Sketchbook of Geoffrey Crayon, gent.* by the immensely popular author Washington Irving. This *Sketchbook* was a fictional series of tales telling of Christmas celebrations in a manor house in England. In Irving's tales, the squire, who is to the manor born, happily invites peasants into his home to celebrate Christmas. These stories provided a heartwarming and positive portrait of people from opposing sides of the class divide mingling together in the spirit of Christmas cheer. To a large extent, real Americans craved a loving Christmas modeled after Irving's fictional English. That yearning became a reality as Irving changed perceptions of Christmas.

It was also about this time that English writer Charles Dickens wrote that beloved masterpiece, *A Christmas Carol*. The story's message of how Christmas symbolized love, charity, generosity, compassion, and kindness, spoke powerfully to English and American alike. There is, however, one respect in which *A Christmas Carol* reflects a Christmas tradition that has not been kept up to the present day: telling spooky stories. Writer Jeffrey Peterson quotes British writer Jerome K. Jerome as observing, "Whenever five or six English-speaking people meet round a fire on Christmas Eve, they start telling each other ghost stories." Although telling ghost stories has pretty much died out as a Christmas custom, the practice has left a its mark through *A Christmas Carol* itself. Watching productions of *A Christmas Carol*, an instructive and inspiring ghost story, are part of modern Christmas practice.

Joel R. Poinsett, an American minister to Mexico, did his bit to encourage Christmas when he brought the poinsettia plant from Mexico to the United States in 1828. This lovely red and green plant fit Christmas perfectly and soon became associated with it.

The Salvation Army contributed to the popularity of Christmas when, in the 1890s, it began sending its own Santa Clauses into the streets to collect donations.

America's Christmas celebration not only became more widespread but much less raucous and far more child-oriented. Special Christmas church services, putting up Christmas trees and decorating them, sending cards, giving gifts, and holding Christmas family dinners became usual in the United States. As America became more influential, these practices spread far and wide across the globe.

Of course, drastic differences in celebrating Christmas remain. For example, some groups celebrate Christmas on a day other than December 25. There are Christian denominations that celebrate Christmas in early January. The Armenian Apostolic Church observes Christmas on January 6. In some Eastern Orthodox Churches, Christmas is celebrated on December 25 – but it falls on a different day than it does in most places because some Greek and Russian Orthodox Churches still use the Julian calendar rather than the Gregorian calendar that is in general international use. Because of this difference in calendars, Christmas can as long occur as long as 13 days after it does in most places. "The date of Christmas (decided on in the 4th century) is always December 25th," states Archimandrite Christódoulos Papadeas of the Greek Orthodox Archdiocese of America. "The Julian (under Julius Caesar) calendar was a bit inaccurate (as to the earth's revolutions around the sun etc.) so a certain Pope Gregory had his leading scientists of the day in 1752 make the correction (which turned out to be a loss of 13 days). The Ecumenical Patriarchate of Constantinople hesitated to adopt the 'new' calendar (then) precisely because the correction was done by the western church. Later however (1921 I believe) the Church (Orthodox) convened and while most adopted the corrected calendar (used universally: secular/commerce), she allowed local churches to make their own decision (to change over or not) while remaining united in dogma and faith (in communion). I reiterate however, the date the Church has set for the celebration of Christmas is 25 December — on whichever calendar." However, that Christmas can be on what is January 7 to most of the world.

In European nations, gifts are usually exchanged on Christmas Eve. In North America, presents are usually opened on the morning of Christmas Day.

In the country of Mexico, in the days leading up to December 25, there are commonly reenactments of the search of Joseph and Mary for a place to stay. In Brazil, Christmas is a summer festival characterized by picnics and fireworks. Brazilians also engage in more sober activities such as priests to church to hold a midnight mass.

Christians are a small minority in India and those who celebrate Christmas substitute mango or bamboo trees for evergreens. The holiday is not widely observed in the predominantly Hindu nation. Japan is also largely non-Christian, with Shinto and Buddhism its most popular faiths. Nonetheless, secular aspects of Christmas such as Christmas trees with decorations and the playing of Christmas songs have become rather popular in that nation as in some others.

However, there may be no country in which Christmas is held more dear than it is in the United States of America. Pew Research has found that 90% of Americans celebrate Christmas.

Chapter 2
A War on Christmas . . . by Jews?

Since the early 2000s, there has been a great deal of public concern about a "War on Christmas." In John Gibson's 2005 book, *The War on Christmas: How the Liberal Plot to Ban the Sacred Christian Holiday is Worse Than You Thought*, Gibson asserts, "Christmas is under attack in such a sustained and strategized manner that there is, no doubt, a war on Christmas."

However, concern that Christmas is being attacked go back much further than the twenty-first century. As Alex Altman noted in his *Time* magazine article on anxieties about this holiday, Henry Ford wrote back in 1921, "The whole record of the Jewish opposition to Christmas . . . shows the venom and directness of [their attack]."

In 1959, the John Birch Society published a pamphlet entitled "There Goes Christmas?!" That pamphlet declared, "One of the techniques now being applied by the Reds to weaken the pillar of religion in our country is the drive to take Christ out of Christmas." That publication also accused "fanatics" at the United Nations of trying to "poison the 1959 Christmas season with their high-pressure propaganda."

Peter Brimelow, an extreme right-wing writer and editor, started a website called VDare.com that ran a competition in 1999 to point out people and institutions making War on Christmas. The Department of Housing and Urban Development was the first focused upon for having a party it called "A Celebration of Holiday Traditions." Indeed, a common thread through the War on Christmas is the nefarious substituting of "holiday" for "Christmas." In 2000, VDare.com pointed to Amazon.com as wronging Christmas through a December greeting of "Happy Holidays!"

Popular conservative pundit Bill O'Reilly has blasted the War on Christmas as "part of the secular progressive agenda" in its attempt "to get Christianity and spirituality out of the public square." O'Reilly's view that Christmas is threatened by the slogan "Happy Holidays" has led him to assert the importance of Christmas specific greetings. Buyers of his book, *A Bold Fresh Piece of Humanity*, received a bumper sticker bearing the phrase: "We Say Merry Christmas."

Anne Graham Lotz, daughter of world famous evangelist Billy Graham and a Bible teacher in her own right, also dislikes the phrase, "Happy Holidays." She asserts, "People just seem to have a problem with Jesus. It's as if people invited you to a birthday party for me but wouldn't let you acknowledge it was for me and my name was blacked out on the invitations. It's CHRIST-mas."

The truth is that there are tensions in America rooted in its valuing of religious freedom which means both the freedom to practice one's religion and the need of our secular government to be neutral as far as supporting or opposing any faith. Those tensions often come to a head in questions involving Christmas. There have been cases in which Christmas practices have been prohibited in government facilities and Christmas decorations removed for Constitutional reasons.

The Salem VA Medical Center sent out an email in 2015 informing its employees that the need to be religion-neutral impacted what could be shown in public areas. That email said, "Displays must not promote any religion. Please note that trees (regardless of the types of ornaments used) have been deemed to promote the Christian religion and will not be permitted in any public areas this year. Employees are permitted to engage in private religious expression in their personal work areas that are not regularly open to the public. Religious expression will be permitted as long as it does not interfere with carrying out of official duties and responsibilities. When the public (veterans and beneficiaries) accesses the Federal workplace, their reasonable impression should be that the government is not sponsoring or endorsing one religion or another."

Marketers often find themselves directly in the crosshairs of the supposed War on Christmas because they want to appeal to the widest number of people possible and that means, for most businesses, keeping the 90% of Americans who celebrate Christmas happy while, at the same, not alienating or offending the other 10%. This marketers' dilemma is exacerbated by the fact that New Year's follows Christmas by just a few days. Some businesses have decided that "Happy Holidays" as a greeting should be a way to please everyone. After all, Christmas is a holiday so it is included along with Chanukah, Kwanzaa, Yule/Winter Solstice, and New Year's. Indeed, one reason for saying "Happy Holidays," is that Christmas and New Year's come so close together that both are included in the greeting — at least for those who celebrate Christmas.

However, to at least some Christmas-loving conservative Christians, "Happy Holidays" degrades and depreciates Christmas. Among the best-known Christian commentators fighting against the alleged War on Christmas are John Gibson, Bill O'Reilly, Rev. Pat Robertson, and Rush Limbaugh. In an article for *The Forward*, Nathaniel Popper wrote that they had been joined in this fight by "several Jewish conservatives, including Rabbi Daniel Lapin, commentator Don Feder and comic Jackie Mason." Another Jew who has taken to the trenches against the anti-Christmas forces is writer Dennis Prager.

Paul Jankowski observes in an article in *Forbes*, "Several retail giants received backlash when they began taking the word Christmas out of their November and December advertising campaigns in an attempt to be politically correct. Lowe's, Home Depot, Sears, Walmart, Target, Best Buy, and GAP have all felt the wrath of believers when they abandoned Christmas for more generic well wishes like 'happy holidays' and Lowe's infamous 'family tree.'"

Christian conservatives are a large group in America and one that is politically and socially active. In the early 2000s, retailers who sought to please everyone with "holiday" ads and signs, found that they had strongly displeased many Christians in what is often called the Religious Right. When conservative Christian organizations let major stores know they felt Christmas was slighted, several companies altered their policies in response to those concerns.

In the early 2000s, "holidays" was very commonly used in signs and advertising by many retail giants. During this period, Bill O'Reilly complained, "About three or four years ago, 'Merry Christmas' began disappearing." However, *The Forward* contacted several chains targeted by activists as slighting Christmas and they all "told *The Forward* that they had not changed their policy on using the word 'Christmas' in advertising campaigns or store decorations in the last five years."

There was controversy in 2005 because retail giant Wal-Mart instructed employees to call out "Happy Holidays" rather than "Merry Christmas" to customers. When someone complained about the "Happy Holidays" greeting, Wal-Mart Customer Service emailed the following incredible reply, "Walmart is a world wide organization and must remain conscious of this. The majority of the world still has different practices other than 'christmas' which is an ancient tradition that has its roots in Siberian shamanism. The colors associated with 'christmas' red and white are actually a representation of the amanita mascera mushroom. Santa is also borrowed from the Caucuses, mistletoe from the Celts, yule log from the Goths, the time from the Visigoth and the tree from the worship of Baal. It is a wide wide world."

Catholic League President Bill Donohue was — understandably — shocked. The email was signed "Kirby." The perplexed Donohue sought clarification from Wal-Mart Senior Manager of Public Relations Dan Fogleman. "As a retailer, we recognize some of our customers may be shopping for Chanukah or Kwanzaa gifts during this time of year and we certainly want these customers in our stores and to feel welcome, just as we do those buying for Christmas," Fogleman stated. "As an employer, we recognize the significance of the Christmas holiday among our family of associates and close our stores in observance, the only day during the year that we are closed."

Donahue did not find Fogleman's answer satisfying. Donahue said it was "nice to know that Walmart is closed on a federal holiday." But he was distressed to find that when he searched the Walmart website for "Hanukkah," 200 items came up; when he searched for "Kwanzaa," 77 items came up; and when he searched for "Christmas," he found a message stating, "We've brought you to our 'Holiday' page based on your search." Calling this "discrimination," the Catholic League called for a boycott of Walmart.

Put on notice about the Catholic League boycott, Fogleman stated that the original reply from "Kirby" was made by a temporary employee who had since been fired. Snipes.com reported that Fogleman stated that Walmart stores, "while encouraging employees to say 'Happy Holidays,' did so to include celebrations from Thanksgiving to Hanukkah, Kwanzaa, and New Year's Eve as well as Christmas."

Walmart issued this statement: "We sincerely apologize to any person or organization that was offended by the inappropriate and inflammatory comments made by this former associate. Wal-Mart is proud to welcome customers of all faiths, and celebrants of all holidays. With more than 138 million customers coming through our stores every week and a variety of holidays that they celebrate throughout this season, 'Happy Holidays' is a pleasant greeting that applies to everyone and every celebration. It's simply our way of wishing our customers a good time with their family and friends during this time of year." Walmart changed its website so searching for "Christmas" popped up a display of Christmas items.

The Catholic League called off its boycott.

In that same year of 2005, the American Family Association (AFA) announced a boycott of Target for downplaying Christmas. Almost 700,000 people signed a "Target boycott" page at the AFA website. Soon after the boycott began, Target released an official statement that included the following: "Over the course of the next few weeks, our advertising, marketing and merchandising will become more specific to the holiday that is approaching—

referring directly to holidays like Christmas and Hanukkah. For example, you will see reference to Christmas in select television commercials, circulars and in-store signage." In early December 2005, AFA Chair Donald W. Wildmon commented, "We are pleased to learn that Target has heard our concerns and decided to use Christmas in their advertising and marketing efforts. Since the company has responded positively, we see no need to continue the boycott."

An Associated Press article in November 2006 observed that Wal-Mart wanted the public to know it had a specifically Christmas spirit: "This holiday season, Wal-Mart isn't trumpeting big bargains only. It's also bringing 'Christmas' back into its marketing, after several years of playing down the term." The piece continued that "several other retailers including Kohl's Corp. and Macy's" were also emphasizing Christmas in response to "mounting criticism from religious groups that staged boycotts against Wal-Mart and other merchants after they eliminated or de-emphasized 'Christmas' in their advertising." Indeed, Wal-Mart announced it was putting on its first "Christmas-specific TV ad in several years" as well as re-naming "Holiday Shops" as "Christmas Shops." Finally, the store stated that the amount of merchandise bearing a "Christmas" rather than "holiday" label would jump by 60%. Kohl's and Macy's were both adopting tactics to ensure they were not seen as slighting Christmas. Kohl's announced it would take care to mention Christmas in print, TV, and radio advertising and Macy's announced that signs specifying "Christmas" would appear in all its department stores. However, the AP reported that Best Buy spokesperson Dawn Bryant related, "We are going to continue to use the term 'holiday' because there are several holidays throughout that time period and we certainly need to be respectful of all of them."

Other retail department store chains altered practices because of AFA complaints. According to a 2005 NewsMax.com article, Sears notified the AFA that "'Merry Christmas' signs have been shipped and are now on display in all its stories. In addition, the retailer notified AFA that the 'Christmas' greeting has also been posted on the Sears.com website." The AFA also received word from Lowe's that its "Holiday Trees" promotion would become a "Christmas Trees" promotion. Walgreens informed the AFA that it was too late to change its printed material for 2005 but that a greater emphasis on Christmas would appear on its 2006 material. "Corporate America is getting the word from the grassroots," Wildmon said.

Concerns about the loss of a specifically Christian spirit have reached the Congress of the United States. In a December 2009 article for CNN.com, Kristi Keck reported, "Republican Rep. Henry Brown of South Carolina introduced a resolution this month asking that the House express support for the use of Christmas symbols and traditions and frown on any attempt to ban references to the holiday." Explaining his motivation, Brown remarked, "Each year I could see a diminishing value of the spiritual part of Christmas. It would seem like another group would go from the Christmas spirit to the holiday spirit."

Not everyone was pleased about the introduction of that resolution. Rev. Barry Lynn is both an ordained minister and Executive Director of Americans United for Separation of Church and State. "Resolutions like this come up because there is this bizarre view by some members of Congress that there is a war on Christmas and that they have to be the generals in some responding army," Rev. Lynn stated. He pointed to the pervasiveness of Christmas in America, observing, "You would literally have to be living in a very deep cave not to understand that there is a religious holiday called Christmas that is soon to come."

According to Keck, "Mathew Staver, law school dean at Liberty University, a Virginia college founded by the late Rev. Jerry Falwell, said, however, that some schools and businesses are going too far to 'censor' Christmas because they don't know the laws. Staver founded the Liberty Counsel, a nonprofit litigation group dedicated to advancing religious freedom and conservative values." Staver believes that an elementary school principal in Oregon who "replaced Christmas trees with snowmen and banned all religious symbols" was an example of someone censoring Christmas because of legal ignorance. Liberty Counsel wrote to the principal to let her know she was not legally obligated to "secularize" Christmas and telling her she was in danger of failing to be "viewpoint neutral" by "banning religious symbols for a holiday with secular components." Staver created a "Naughty & Nice" list about retailers who do/don't include Christmas references in their ads.

The Family Research Council (FRC) is a conservative Christian organization that is concerned about Christmas. According to FRC Senior Fellow for Policy Studies Peter Sprigg, "Political correctness is preventing people from even saying 'Merry Christmas.'" Sprigg asserts, "If we want to be concerned about the fact that we are a multicultural nation, then the solution is to allow everyone the freedom to celebrate what they want rather than stifling the celebration of the majority because it might be offensive to the minority."

In 2013, GAP & Old Navy changed their "holiday" marketing policy and sent a letter to the AFA stating that they would now use the expression "Merry Christmas." The letter stated, "As a global retailer, we embrace the diversity of our customers and respect a variety of traditions and faiths during the holidays, including Christmas. Starting today, every Gap Outlet window will have signs that say 'Merry Christmas' along with Christmas trees and wreaths throughout their stores."

There have been several court challenges to aspects of Christmas celebration in government run institutions such as the public schools. In 2015, a Concord High School student and his father in Elkhart, Indiana, together with the Freedom From Religion Foundation (FFRF) filed a lawsuit challenging the constitutionality of a segment of the school's annual "Christmas Spectacular." That segment was a 20 minute enactment of the nativity.

U.S. District Court Judge Jon Deguilio granted a preliminary injunction forbidding that nativity enactment. FFRF asserted, "It is illegal for a public school to endorse religion to students by organizing a religious performance such as acting out the exclusively Christian legend of Jesus' birth. The performance has a clearly devotional message and thus would be appropriate in a church setting but not in a public school."

In his decision, Judge Deguilio stated, "The Plaintiffs are likely to succeed on the merits own their claim that the inclusion of the living nativity scene in the show as currently proposed violate the Establishment Clause." He also said, "The nativity scene is emphasized in a manner unlike any other aspect of the show" and "conveys solemnity and reverence, as if the audience is being asked to venerate the nativity, not simply acknowledge or appreciate its place in the winter holiday season."

Reporter Joel Porter wrote, "The school district argued that a live Nativity scene on school grounds isn't necessarily unconstitutional but rather that it depends on the context." Porter also quoted parents and students expressing sadness at the decision. One parent commented, "Disappointed to see Christ taken out of Christmas. Truly, that is the reason why we celebrate it." A Concord student, Janae Hall, remarked, "I find it very odd, because you don't have to go, and you don't have to be a part of it if you don't want to be a part of it."

Pointing the finger at the Jewish anti-Christmas Culprit

Just *who* is making War on Christmas? The suggested villains vary. Secularists and liberals are probably the most commonly cited miscreants in the mainstream press.

However, some have another candidate: Jews. As already mentioned, Henry Ford wrote about Jewish anti-Christmas activity way back in the 1920s.

One of the people pushing hardest on this accusation is the famous — some would say infamous — David Duke. It should be noted that, in interviews with mainstream press representatives, Duke often complains that his interviewer makes much too much of his youthful leadership of a Ku Klux Klan group. He argues that it is unfair to emphasize this as he left that Klan organization more than forty years ago. He also points out that, while there have been Klan groups that committed violent acts including murders, he has never even been accused, much less convicted, of any violent crime. Moreover, he does not advocate violence against any racial or ethnic group and adamantly states that he has never done so.

Nevertheless, it is not unreasonable for people to recall Duke's youthful stint as "Grand Wizard" of a Klan group since that is how he first came to national prominence. Part of the reason Klansman David Duke grabbed so much attention was that he was a then-young man who was both handsome and clean-cut and who advocated a "new" Ku Klux Klan that was media savvy — and non-violent.

Duke brought other changes into his KKK organization. The Klan had generally been all-male with women having their own associated all-female organization. Duke welcomed women into his Klan and allowed them full membership.

Additionally, Duke's KKK was no longer limited to Protestants. He invited Roman Catholics to join his Klan — and at least some Catholics accepted the invitation. Back in the 1970s, when he appeared on *Both Sides Now*, a short-lived TV talk show co-hosted by conservative George Putnam and liberal Mort Sahl, Putnam brought up the KKK's history of anti-Catholicism. "We've got nothing against Catholics," Duke retorted. "We've got Catholic members." Much more recently, Wolf Blitzer interviewed Duke. When introducing the guest, Blitzer prominently featured Duke's KKK connection and mentioned the Klan's anti-Catholic history. "At least get your facts right," Duke said. "I've never made an anti-Catholic statement in my life." Indeed, to this author's knowledge, he never has.

Jews are a different story. And while he has moderated his message as he has aged, the man *Time* magazine called "Mr. White" on a cover story, has always stoutly excluded Jews, regardless of their physical characteristics, from the "white" race.

Indeed, the "race" of Jews forms something of a puzzle since "Jew" describes a category that is both ethnicity and religion. One Jew described the situation by saying, "If you were an atheist, you'd just be atheist. If I was an atheist, I'd still be a Jew." Since anyone can convert to the religion of Judaism, there are Jews of sub-Saharan African ancestry, Native American ancestry, and Asian ancestry. But if a person of Jewish ethnicity converts to another faith, that person remains ethnically Jewish. Thus, there are ethnic Jews of all faiths and non-faiths; there are people of all ethnic/racial groups who are religiously Jewish.

The majority of Jews tend to be either Ashkenazi or Sephardic Jews, the former having the appearance of Western/Eastern/Northern Europeans and the latter of Southern Europeans. Most Jews have fair complexions, round eyes, lips that are relatively thin, and hair that may be straight or curly but is unlikely to be as tightly curled as that of people of sub-Saharan African lineage, and that ranges in color with Jews having blonde, red, brown, and black hair. A characteristic popularly associated with Jews — and common in many European ethnicities as well as in Middle Eastern people and in some Native American and North African groups — is a nose that has a large or hooked bridge. Although, as just pointed out, the trait is often seen in some non-white groups, it is possible to see this as a kind of exaggerated Caucasian characteristics since the general tendency is for sub-Saharan Africans, Asians, and Native Americans to have low-bridged noses.

Yet even a sour cream pale, blonde or red-haired, and blue or green-eyed Jew — of which the world has many — is non-white to David Duke and many, probably most, others in the "white supremacist," "white separatist" or "white nationalist" camps.

To them, these white-looking non-whites wage a battle against a holiday most Christians cherish. On David Duke's website, he posted a drawing of a Grinch with the Israeli flag on his torso and a Star of David on his hat. The title of an article on the subject by Duke is "The Jewish War on Christmas!" He contends that "a long war" has been and is being "waged against Christmas by the Jewish establishment in the media, the courts, and the political arena."

In early December 2016, Duke ran a piece on his website decrying "The Jewish War on Christmas!" This Jewish war on Christmas is represented by "Christmas Symbols Banned While Jewish Symbols Erected Across America!" He calls on people to "defend" Christmas from the Jewish onslaught. He asserts, "The leading Jewish organizations of the United States led the fight to ban Christian Christmas tradition on public ground." He argues that Jewish organizations have successfully fought to "restrict the mention of Christmas" by substituting expressions like "Winter Holidays and Winter Break." The entertainment industry comes in for special criticism in Duke's essay: "Jewish Hollywood continues to produce films and TV programs that defile our European Christmas traditions. Even the venerable figure of Santa Claus or St. Nicklaus has not escaped Jewish hate."

Two years later, in 2018, Duke published a piece decrying "How an Ultra-Racist Zio-Grinch Stole" Christmas. It was illustrated with a cartoon of the Dr. Seuss Grinch with an Israeli flag across his belly and a Star of David on his hat. He contrasted "Christmas Symbols Banned" with "Monster Menorahs Erected." He calls Jews "a strange and powerful, alien Grinch who stole Christmas." Duke further writes, "Rich and powerful Jewish groups like the American Jewish Committee, the ADL and the Jewish run and financed ACLU waged war on Christmas." He asserts that he and others will continue to fight the "arrogant Jewish tyrants [who] think they have won."

There are others who single out Jews as battling against the Christmas holiday. One example is a curious character who calls himself Brother Nathanael. Born Milton Kapner in a Jewish family, young Milton appears to have had a somewhat troubled childhood. In particular, there is an incident that he mentions to this day as having badly shook him. As a child, Milton's parents allowed him to sing Christmas carols with his Gentile chums during the season. One evening, an adult neighbor pointed to him and snarled, "What's a Jew-boy like you doing singing Christmas carols?" Embarrassed and upset, little Milton ran home to his parents. He said to his father, "Why don't we Jews accept Jesus Christ?" Dad replied, "Son, it is fine to sing Christmas carols but you were born a Jew and you will stay a Jew." As he grew into adulthood, he became increasingly disillusioned by Judaism. He converted to Christianity. He apparently explored different denominations before settling on Eastern Orthodoxy, specifically the Russian Orthodox Church Outside Russia (ROCOR). He spent time in monasteries as a novice but never actually became a monk although he now dresses like one.

This curious converted Christian formed The Brother Nathanael Foundation, described on its website as "a tax-exempt non-profit corporation, dedicated to the promotion of Christian principles in American society." He routinely issues anti-Semitic statements in his "Real Jew News" reports which usually consist of articles neither "real" nor "news" but that just attack Jewish people.

It is important to mention that Brother Nathanael's activities are not supported by the church to which he belongs. A "Statement from the Chancery of the ROCOR Synod of Bishops" addressed his activities, stating, "The clergymen and laity of the Russian Church Abroad are hereby informed that the actions of Nathanael (Kapner) do not have the blessing of the Synod of Bishops. Profoundly saddened by the state of his soul, we call upon Nathanael (Kapner) to refrain from posting on the Internet, to a life of repentance in Christ 'where there is neither Greek nor Jew, circumcision nor uncircumcision, Barbarian, Scythian, bond nor free: but Christ is all and in all (Colossians 3:11).'"

Although Kapner is a prominent anti-Semite, some of his fellow anti-Semites often do not support him because he is ethnically Jewish. On the *Total Fascism* website, anti-Semite Andrew Anglin states, "I will say that first and foremost my opposition to him is because he is a biological Jew."

Brother Nathanael is a strong proponent of the idea that those of Hebrew origin are determined to gut Christmas. In his "Real Jew News," he runs headlines like "ADL's Jewish War on Christmas," "A CHRISTmas Hating Jew Is Foiled!" and "How The Jews Stole Christmas," and "The Jewish War On Christmas."

Although most people who push the idea of a "War on Christmas" do not openly point the finger at those of Hebrew ancestry, some commentators see the concept as rooted in bigotry against Jews. Dan Rosenberg penned an article making this case entitled "The Anti-Semitic Roots of 'The War On Christmas.'" Rosenberg argues that the "War on Christmas" is among "bigoted buzzwords" such as "New York lawyers (and bankers)," "Hollywood culture," "secularists," and "internationalists," — all of which Rosenberg believes are code terms for Jews. He points out that while President Donald Trump proudly proclaimed, "People are saying Merry Christmas again," the truth is that it never disappeared: "Former U.S. President Barack Obama said it, as did all of his predecessors. People in stores say it, greeting cards say it, even Jews have been known to say it when dealing with Christians over the holiday season."

Another Jewish writer, Matthew Rozsa, also asserts that the idea of a "War on Christmas" is fundamentally bigoted, pointing to its roots in the anti-Semitic writings of Henry Ford. He quotes Ford stating, "It is not religious tolerance in the midst of religious difference, but religious attack that they preach and practice. The whole record of Jewish opposition to Christmas, Easter and certain patriotic songs shows that." Rozsa elaborates that Ford asserted that "American rights have been interfered with, and the interference has been made with the assistance of their own broadmindedness." Furthermore, Rozsa believes that this could be said by "War on Christmas" concerned people today if "political correctness" were substituted for "broadmindedness."

Are Jews waging war on Christmas? If so, they face an extraordinary amount of subversion within their own ranks. The truth is that Jews have made, and continue to make, wonderful contributions to the celebration of Christmas. In fact, at least in the modern era, it is possible that Jews have done more to enrich the celebration of this special day than any other ethnic/faith group! The purpose of this book is to show just how much Christmas has benefited from Jewish contributions.

Perhaps there is no clearer and stronger evidence for this than what Jews have done in creating Christmas songs and contributing to Christmas movies.

Chapter 3
Christmas Songs Written and/or Composed by Jews

This chapter is devoted to some of the most popular Christmas tunes which were either written or co-written by Jewish people. It does not claim to cover every Christmas tune written or co-written by a Jew. However, it discusses some of our most cherished Christmas tunes that had Jewish lyricists and/or composers, the stories behind the songs, and the backgrounds of their Jewish creators or co-creators. It also discusses the background of the Gentiles who, in some cases, collaborated with Jews to craft such songs. As we shall see, some of our most popular Christmas songs are the product of Jewish and Gentile cooperation.

A "White Christmas" and the Man who Dreamed It

"Irving Berlin has no place in American music — he is American music," renowned composer Jerome Kern famously proclaimed. Kern spoke with reason. Irving Berlin, a gifted Jewish-American, was one of the most prolific and gifted composers and lyricists in the history of the world. This prodigious songwriter authored such musical standards as "Alexander's Ragtime Band," "How Deep Is The Ocean," "Anything You Can Do," "There's No Business

Like Show Business," "Puttin' On The Ritz," "A Pretty Girl Is Like A Melody," "Heat Wave," "Easter Parade," "God Bless America" —and, the reason for his inclusion in this volume — the beloved "White Christmas." He contributed mightily to theater and film scores.

Like so many Americans in the "nation of immigrants," Berlin was not born in the United States. He was born in Czarist Russia on May 11, 1888 as Israel Beilin. His father was a "cantor"— the synagogue official who sings the religious songs and leads the congregation in prayer during a service —in a Russian synagogue so it is likely Israel had musical talents in his genes that were nurtured by his environment into musical skills.

Rob Kapilow, in an article for *The Star*, writes, "When Alexander II, the great Russian reformer who freed the serfs, was assassinated in 1881, his son Alexander III ascended to the throne. It quickly became clear that his repressive regime would do everything it could to undo his father's liberal reforms and stigmatize the Jews. According to one of Alexander's closest advisors, the hope was that 'one third of the Jews will convert, one third will die, and one third will flee the country." In the book *Write On, Irving Berlin!* Leslie Kimmelman states, "It was a bad time and place to be Jewish. Gangs of angry men rode from village to village in pogroms, destroying Jewish homes and hurting the people who lived in them." As a small child, little Israel Beilin had to helplessly watch as his family's house was burned down before his eyes by anti-Semitic thugs.

The Beilin family were among many Jews who decided to leave their homeland during the reign of Czar Alexander III. By that time, there were seven children in the Beilin family. One of the children was already married. The entire family left Russia. Like many others leaving Russia, the family selected the United States as their new home. Little Israel Beilin was five years old when his family journeyed to New York in 1893, making their first stop at Ellis Island, before settling into an impoverished but robust and growing Jewish neighborhood in the Lower East Side. Israel was nicknamed "Izzy" and his father continued working as a cantor in this community. Life was rough and the financially struggling family lived in a crowded tenement.

Izzy quickly picked up English but did not make a positive impression on his teachers. As Kimmelman notes, teachers complained that "he daydreams too much" and "sings to himself."

As was common among many immigrants, Israel Beilin soon changed his name. According to *The Guardian* — as reprinted in the "White Christmas" page of the Hymns and Carols website, he "named himself after an English actor and German city." Name changing was common among immigrants who often wanted a name that would be easier for native English speakers to pronounce. In addition, some people — Jews among them — wanted a name that would not immediately make their ethnicity known. Finally, people of all ethnicities often change their names when they go into the entertainment business because they want a name that sounds "better" or more appropriate for their persona. This is one reason Marion Morrison is known to the public as John Wayne; his birth name has a rather intellectual, even effete, ring to it while his two-syllable entertainment industry name sounds simple, strong, and decisively masculine.

Izzy's father died when the boy was only 13. The loss of the family breadwinner led the youngster to work a variety of odd jobs including singing on the streets as a busker for change. America's robust ethnic diversity is underlined in the life of this Jewish immigrant from Russia who did a stint as a singing waiter in a Chinatown eatery.

Recognition for his musical talents came early. He published his first tune, "Marie from Sunny Italy," in 1907. In 1911, he catapulted to glory with an international hit, "Alexander's Ragtime Band," a tune not technically of the ragtime genre but one that paid sprightly tribute to the ragtime craze. The sales of the song made Irving Berlin financially successful and won him widespread recognition in the entertainment industry.

Things were indeed looking up for Berlin in 1912 when he married his sweetheart, a woman named Dorothy Goetz. The newlyweds honeymooned in Cuba — and then tragedy struck. She came down with typhoid fever and died only six months after the wedding. According to writer Laurence Masion, "Devastated, Berlin slowed his pace considerably, but turned his sorrow into 'When I Lost You,' a veritable haiku of grief, which critics agree matured Berlin into a major songwriter."

In 1917, apparently recovered from his grief, he founded his own publishing house, Irving Berlin Music, Inc. Irving Berlin became a naturalized citizen of the United States in 1918. Later that same year, he was drafted into his adopted country's Army. The musician did not adapt well to military life. "I found out quickly I wasn't much of a soldier," he recalled. "There were a lot of things about army life that I didn't like, and the thing I didn't like most of all was reveille. I hated it. I hated it so much I used to lie awake nights thinking about how much I hated it."

It should not be shocking that the music-minded man was not cut out for military life. It should also not be shocking that his sentiments found their way into a song. "Oh! How I Hate to Get Up in the Morning" was Berlin's anti-tribute to the life of a soldier. Despite Berlin's negativity toward the army, he was promoted to sergeant. A superior officer, Major General J. Franklin Bell, asked Berlin to "put on a little show" for his fellow soldiers. Berlin agreed and crafted a series of songs for that show: "I Can Always Find a Little Sunshine in the YMCA," "Kitchen Police," and "Dream On, Little Soldier Boy."

Berlin wrote a song for the revue that he eventually decided not to include: "God Bless America." It was too serious and would not fit in with the other songs he had composed for this rather irreverent musical revue. As was his custom, he did not destroy the song but laid it aside. The show that he created was a riotous musical comedy entitled *Yip! Yip! Yaphank!* It was first performed in July 1918 at the Liberty Theatre of Camp Upton. Just a month later, it was performed at the Century Theatre in New York City. An appreciative reporter wrote, "It may well be that no mortal theatre was ever so beautiful as the Century that hot night on August of 1918, and it is even more likely that no mortal show could ever have been quite so transcendentally wonderful, so altogether out of this world."

After the end of "The Great War," also called "The War To End All Wars" (Oops! Did not quite work out that way, did it?), and Berlin's military service, he went great gangbusters on Broadway. He authored the entire score of the famous *Ziegfeld Follies of 1919* that included such beloved Ziegfeld standards as Berlin's "A Pretty Girl is Like a Melody." Laurence Maison reports, "Berlin struck out on his own as a producer. With veteran Broadway entrepreneur Sam H. Harris, he built the Music Box Theatre on West 45th Street as a venue for his own work." In 1921, he started producing musical revues at the Music Box Theatre, introducing tunes like "Say It With Music" and What'll I Do?"

The great Berlin's protean talents were put to good use for the glorious comedy of the Marx Brothers when Berlin collaborated with George S. Kaufman to compose *The Cocoanuts*, a hit musical that would eventually be filmed in sound in 1929.

In 1924, the widower became enamored of socialite and writer Ellin Mackay. His affection was returned. He wrote a song especially for her entitled "Always." However, Ellin Mackay was of Irish descent and the Roman Catholic faith. Thus, there was a bit of "Romeo and Juliet" to this romance that crossed ethnic and religious lines. Ellin Mackay's father was the wealthy financier Clarence Mackay. Clarence's father, and Ellin's paternal grandfather, was John William Mackay, who had immigrated to America from Ireland and made a fortune as head of a silver mining corporation. Clarence Mackay piled even more riches onto the family fortune through shrewd investing in the then-young fields of telegraph and radio. Indeed, he was President of the Mackay Radio and Telegraph Company as well as Board Chair of the Postal Telegraph and Cable Corporation. Affluent beyond the average person's dreams, Clarence Mackay was outraged that his daughter would marry a Jew. Clarence Mackay disinherited Ellin and barred her from entering his home, after her January 4, 1926 marriage to Irving Berlin. For Ellin, who had always been close to her father, this was an emotionally crushing blow.

Nevertheless, the marriage was strong and the implicit promise Berlin made in the song "Always" was kept on both sides as this marriage would last more than sixty years — until "death did them part" as is usually said in traditional marriage vows. However, the pain caused by her father's action may have been cushioned by the joy she and Irving experienced when Ellin gave birth later that same year to her first child, a daughter.

The scandal of his interfaith/interethnic marriage had hardly dampened Berlin's talents as he composed for the full score of the *Ziegfeld Follies of 1927*.

In late 1928, Berlin's personal life was again suffused with joy: his son was born. Ellin and Irving named the boy Irving Berlin, Jr. Only weeks after the baby's birth, on December 25 — Christmas Day — 1928, the infant died. The exact reason for the very untimely death remains obscure. Berlin and his wife were, of course, devastated by grief. Perhaps the only good thing about this heartbreaking tragedy was that Ellin heard from her father for the first time since their estrangement as he sent a condolence letter to his grieving daughter. However, there were people who heaped insult upon injury as Laurence Bergreen reports in *As Thousands Cheer: The Life of Irving Berlin:* "The bereaved parents also heard, amid the conventional expressions of sympathy, anti-Semitic remarks occasioned by the death. Since the child had died on Christmas morning, a few of Ellin's former friends whispered, 'It's God's punishment for marrying a Jew.'"

For many years after the death of Irving Berlin, Jr., while much of the world was joyfully celebrating Merry Christmas, Berlin and Ellin would somberly visit their child's grave on December 25.

Two other children, both daughters, would be born to the Berlins in following years.

The infamous Stock Market Crash of 1929 to a large extent wiped out the fortune of Clarence Mackay. Bergreen states, "He had the hideous distinction of incurring the largest loss suffered by an individual in the Crash." Mackay had to sell the thoroughbred horses he loved, auction off an extensive art collection, and fire his staff of 134 servants. In what must have seemed crushing humiliation, he moved out of his mansion and into what had formerly been the cottage of the estate's gatekeeper. The grand country estate of Clarence Mackay had been named Harbor Hill; in the aftermath of financial ruin, it acquired the nickname "Heartbreak House."

Many people may have been surprised that Mackay's longtime mistress, Anna Case, stood by him even as his fortune turned to dust. No gold digger, she married the financially ruined man on July 18, 1931. Many people were also surprised than Ellin Berlin attended this wedding — and shocked that Irving Berlin was there.

By the time of his second wedding, Mackay was not only impoverished but dying of the throat cancer that would eventually claim his life. His declining years were made relatively comfortable because the son-in-law he had shunned, the man whose love for Mackay's daughter had led him to disinherit her, reached out to him with a gift of about a million dollars! This generous gift did not mean Mackay regained his former position but it meant he lived in relative comfort while receiving his medical treatments until the cancer killed him in 1938. Mackay's attitude toward his Jewish son-in-law was thawed by the latter's generous expression of forgiveness and caring.

While many previously wealthy people were turned into paupers by the Depression, Irving Berlin suffered relatively minor losses. Indeed, throughout this sad period in the country's history, Berlin continued to prosper as he graced Broadway with productions like *Face the Music* and teamed up with Moss Hart to create the classic revue *As Thousands Cheer*. Indeed, Berlin continued to enjoy both prosperity and productivity during the Depression years.

Like many people worldwide, especially Jewish people, Berlin watched with alarm as Adolf Hitler and his Nazi Party came to power in Germany. During the late 1930s, it was unclear as to whether or not the United States was destined for conflict with Hitler but it was apparent that ominous forces were brewing in Europe. In 1938, Berlin decided to write something that would give musical form to his love for his adopted nation. He worked on new songs but found himself disappointed in them. "It then occurred to me to reexamine the old song, 'God Bless America,'" he would state.

America should be grateful that he did. He changed some of the lyrics. For example, the original read, "Stand beside her and guide her to the right with a light from above." He altered this to "through the night with a light from above." The line, "Make her victorious on land and foam, God bless America, my home, sweet home," became "From the mountains to the prairies to the oceans white with foam, God bless America, my home, sweet home."

Looking around for the right singer to introduce "God Bless America," Berlin hit upon the enormously gifted Kate Smith who first sang this beautiful tune over the radio on November 11, 1938. Bergreen writes, "Within days of its belated debut, the song began to acquire the status of an unofficial national anthem."

A few years after Berlin bestowed the incomparable "God Bless America" on his countrymen and women, the makers of the musical comedy *Holiday Inn* (1942) asked Berlin to write a song about each major holiday of the year. The plot of the film was about a performing trio consisting of a singer named Jim Hardy, a dancer named Ted Hanover, and a singer-dancer named Lila Dixon. The group broke up because Lila broke her engagement with fiancé Jim to marry Ted. Jim leaves show business to work a Connecticut farm. Farming does not work out; indeed, he is so broken by it he must recuperate in a sanitarium! After recovering, he decides to open an inn that will be open only on holidays — thus, the name *Holiday Inn*. In the black and white film, Bing Crosby plays Jim Hardy, Fred Astaire plays Ted Hanover, and Virginia Dale plays Lila Dixon. A fourth major character, Linda Mason, who becomes a second love interest for Jim Hardy, is played by Marjorie Reynolds.

Steven Lewis, in The Bing Crosby Internet Museum, comments, "Berlin, who was Jewish, found that writing a song about Christmas was the most challenging." It is likely that it was made even more challenging because this holiday was so intimately connected with one of the most lacerating experiences of Berlin's life — the death of his infant son.

However, it should also be noted that, although Berlin was Jewish, living in a country in which the majority of people are Christian meant that he was exposed to this holiday celebration and, thus, had experience — albeit observed experience — upon which to draw for the song. As Bergreen writes, Berlin "had nostalgic memories of childhood Christmases on the Lower East Side, and especially of the Christmas tree belonging to his neighbors, the

O'Haras." Oddly, being in Los Angeles, California — a place in which snow is rare even in December — helped inspire Berlin to write the tune that would make history: "The palm trees and heat only made him yearn for cold weather and snow. What he wanted, what everybody wanted, was a white Christmas." He had it! As Bergreen observes, "With a subject as potent and evocative as Christmas, a few well-chosen words and images spoke volumes."

Indeed they did.

There is a beautiful combination of joy and nostalgia in "White Christmas." Yet there is also a touch of sadness — which makes it all the more powerful. Jody Rosen, author of a book entitled *White Christmas: The Story of an American Song*, has speculated, "The kind of deep secret of the song may be that it was Berlin responding in some way to his melancholy about the death of his son."

In 1941, Berlin auditioned the song before Bing Crosby who assured Berlin that the tune was good. However, it was not the *Holiday Inn* song that Berlin expected to make the biggest impression. In *The Christmas Carol Reader*, Will Studwell reports that before the film came out, "the expected hit of Berlin's score was to be the Valentine's Day song, 'Be Careful, It's My Heart.' That song quickly lost out to 'White Christmas' and has more or less been relegated to the status of a historical footnote in comparison to its highly celebrated score mate."

"White Christmas" was introduced to the general public on December 25, 1941, when Crosby sang it on his radio program, the *Kraft Music Hall*. Writing for *Country Living*, Taysha Murtaugh asserts that the carol is "soulful, longing, and sad, but especially so at the time. Pearl Harbor had been attacked just a few weeks before." The tune spoke powerfully to an audience whose country was under attack, who knew the entire world was in jeopardy due to the aggression of the Axis Powers that included not only Hirohito's Japan but Nazi Germany and Fascist Italy, and which nevertheless celebrated the beloved and cherished holiday of Christmas.

Crosby recorded "White Christmas" on a record on May 29, 1942. Movie theater audiences were treated to it when the black and white motion picture

Holiday Inn was released only a few months later in August 1942. The song won the Academy Award for Best Song of 1942.

Bing Crosby often toured with the USO to entertain America's troops and had mixed feelings about singing "White Christmas." Crosby said, "I hesitated about doing it because invariably it caused such a nostalgic yearning among the men that it made them sad. Heaven knows, I didn't come that far to make them sad. For this reason, several times I tried to cut it out of the show but these guys just hollered for it." Understandably so because young men away from home to risk life and limb for their country knew that its lyrics spoke the feelings that were so strongly written on their hearts.

Lewis writes, "Bing's single of 'White Christmas' sold more than 30 million copies worldwide and was recognized as the best-selling single in any music category for more than 50 years until 1998 when Elton John's tribute to Princess Diana, 'Candle in the Wind,' overtook it in a matter of months. However, Bing's recording of 'White Christmas' has sold additional millions of copies as part of numerous albums, including his best-selling album 'Merry Christmas,' which was first released as an L.P. in 1949."

In the decades since the tune debuted, it has been recorded in a variety of languages including Dutch, Yiddish, Japanese, and Swahili. It has been covered by a wildly disparate group of performers including Elvis Presley, Karen Carpenter, Bette Midler, and Lady Gaga. Murtaugh reports, "With 50 million copies sold" the recording of "White Christmas" by Bing Crosby is "the best-selling Christmas song of all time."

In an article for *The Star*, Rob Kapilow notes, "Before Irving Berlin's 'White Christmas' — sung by Bing Crosby — broke sales records in 1942, composers had spent little time on Christmas songs because it seemed their appeal could only be seasonal." The success of Berlin's now-standard Christmas tune alerted other composers and songwriters that writing Christmas songs could make for financial success and popular appreciation.

In the post-war years, Irving Berlin continued to craft hit after hit, contributing on multiple levels to America's burgeoning entertainment industry. Maslon reports, "The relative prosperity of Cold War America also provided subjects for Berlin's satirical perspective: 'They Like Ike' from *Call Me Madam* (1950) eventually became a theme song for Eisenhower's successful presidential campaign in 1952." He went on to write the full score for the 1962 Broadway play, *Mr. President.*

Maslon elaborates, "In 1968, he was honored by a 90-minute-long tribute in primetime on *The Ed Sullivan Show* (where he sang 'God Bless America' backed up by a phalanx of Boy Scouts)." For the next decades, the wealthy aging man led a quieter life, occasionally writing lyrics and giving interviews. In 1988, Ellin died at 85. Irving died on September 22, 1989 at the age of 101.

Although Irving Berlin wrote the single song that is the most popular Christmas tune, he was neither the first nor last Jew to make a significant musical contribution to this quintessentially Christian holiday. One whose contribution came before Berlin's will be discussed in the next section.

The Wonder of "Winter Wonderland"

In Ace Collins' book *Stories Behind the Greatest,* Collins asserts, "'Winter Wonderland' may be the only holiday song that owes its magical, upbeat lyrics to a devastating terminal disease." This magical song of true wonder was the result of artistic cooperation between Gentile and Jew.

The lyricist of "Winter Wonderland" was a Gentile, Richard "Dick" Smith, who was born in 1901 in Honesdale, Pennsylvania. He grew up as one of the four children of John H. Smith, a partner in a cut glass manufacturing plant who served on the Episcopal Church Vestry, and Eliza Bruning Smith, a homemaker. In an article for *The News Eagle*, Peter Becker writes about Smith's childhood days in Honesdale, remarking, "One-horse open sleighs were not yet nostalgic images for calendars or Christmas cards but were still a way people got about, especially in the countryside in those winter days" when the area was thick with snow.

Smith suffered tragedy early and Becker writes that the boy was "about age 7 or 8 when his father died."

The boy showed musical interest and acumen from an early age. An upright piano graced the Smith home and young Dick made good use of it. Becker reports that a classmate named Margaret Kreitner Morrison recalled that he "showed a gift for the piano from his school days" and also observed, "Dick was witty and clever at making verses."

Ten of his songs were published in the 1930s including tunes like "The Breeze That's Bringing My Honey Back To Me," "I Thrill When They Mention Your Name" and "Tumbleweed."

While still a child, Smith contracted tuberculosis. As an adult, he spent a large amount of time at the West Mountain Sanitarium in Scranton, Pennsylvania. It was on a winter's day at the sanitarium that he looked out a window and saw children playing in the snow, happily building figures made of snow, and light-heartedly throwing snowballs at each other. Inspired by the sight, Smith went to a table and wrote a poem that was romantic, slightly humorous, and filled with the joy of Christmas — even though Christmas is never actually mentioned.

The story told is a tad ambiguous. References to "Parson Brown" and getting married would indicate the narrator is a young adult. But the lines about having "lots of fun with mister snowman" and the "other kids" knocking him down suggests our narrator is a child. Perhaps we are ultimately meant to think the narrator is a child with a childhood sweetheart and they are making believe that they will wed. Or that they are adults planning to wed but retaining enough childlikeness to play with snowman. Or perhaps we do not need to "over think" the lines of the song but should just enjoy its lovely and light-hearted beauty — a light-hearted beauty made poignant by the knowledge that it was written by a sick man in a sanitarium.

References to sleigh bells ringing and snow glistening immediately transport us to winter and make winter the time of a snowy "wonderland." It might be politically incorrect in today's world to talk about "the Eskimo way" as one of "frolic and play." However, it is possible that these words do not indicate that Eskimos/Inuit people "frolic and play" more than other people but that, since everyone enjoys frolicking and playing, we all do it "the Eskimo way" when the environment is akin to the all-year-round snowy environment of that particular ethnic group.

Shortly after putting this lovely poem down on paper, the Gentile Smith showed the lyrics to his Jewish friend, professional pianist, conductor, and composer Felix Bernard.

Felix Bernard had been born Felix Bernhardt in 1897 in New York City. Like Smith, Bernard showed musical promise from an early age. By his teenage years, he was already a professional pianist. He would also enjoy success as a tap dancer and the leader of his own band. Find A Grave reports, "His first taste of success was with 'Dardanella' (1919), co-written with Johnny S. Black and Fred Fisher, and one of the first records to sell 1 million copies." During his lifetime, Bernard wrote one-act vaudeville comedies and produced material for some of the top performers of the day including Sophie Tucker, Eddie Cantor, Al Jolson, and Marilyn Miller. He wrote or co-wrote many popular songs, among them "You Opened My Eyes," "Cutest Kid in Town," and "I'd Rather Be Me."

Bernard wrote the music for Smith's poem. "Winter Wonderland" was recorded by *Guy Lombardo and His Royal Canadians* and garnered second place on 1934's Hit Parade. Sadly, Smith died the next year, in 1936, when he was only 34.

"Winter Wonderland" receded from popular view until 1946 when it was recorded in rival versions by the Andrews Sisters and by Perry Como. By then, neither of its writers was there to enjoy its popularity as Bernard passed away in 1944 at the age of 47.

In the decades since Como and the Andrews Sisters battled it out with competing versions of the tune, "Winter Wonderland" has become a Christmas standard.

Santa Claus is Comin' to Town

Another of several examples of Gentile-Jewish collaboration, "Santa Claus is Comin' To Town" had its lyrics composed by Gentile Haven Gillespie and its tune composed by Jewish J. Fred Coots. The first singer to publicly sing the tune was the Jewish Eddie Cantor, who let loose with the song on his radio program in November 1934.

Haven Gillespie came into the world in 1888 in Covington, Kentucky. At the age of 16, he dropped out of high school and found work as a typesetter at Cincinnati's *Times Star* newspaper. When in his 20s, he moved to New York City. *The New York Times* hired him as a reporter. Then he began writing lyrics for vaudeville and started working for Tin Pan Alley. However, as Jason Ankeny relates on the Allmusic website, "[He] held onto his day job for a number of years, ultimately maintaining his membership in the International Typographic Union until his death." Early in his adulthood, he established a reputation as a great Tin Pan Alley songwriter, penning such numbers as "Drifting and Dreaming," "Honey," "By the Sycamore Tree," and "You Go To My Head." He collaborated with many big names including Henry Marshall, Harry Tobias, Charles Tobias, Dick Whiting, and Rudy Vallee.

In 1934, song publisher Leo Feist met in his office with Gillespie. Feist wanted Gillespie to compose a children's Christmas song. The songwriter was notably unenthusiastic about such a project but Feist insisted he had a "good vocabulary" for children's songs. Gillespie agreed to try. Some fifteen minutes later, Gillespie was on the subway and he wrote the lyrics to the classic "Santa Claus is Comin' to Town. Later he took the lyrics to J. Frederick Coots, who needed a mere ten minutes to compose music for it.

Coots was born in 1897 in New York City. His mother taught him to play the piano. In his early adulthood, he worked in a bank on Wall Street. In 1914, he felt a call to music. He worked as a professional pianist and did stocking in a music store. After his first song was published in 1917, he went into vaudeville. He played piano and wrote songs for major performers including the legendary Sophie Tucker. He wrote songs and performed until his 1985 death. Coots died a decade after Gillespie who passed away in 1975.

Eddie Cantor, at the insistence of his wife Ida, debuted the song on the Thanksgiving special of the *Eddie Cantor Show*. "Santa Claus is Comin' to Town" was an instant hit. An article by Tom Eames on the Song Lists website relates, "The morning after the radio show, there were orders for 100,000 copies of sheet music and by Christmas, sales had passed 400,000." The first known recording of the song was on October 24, 1924 by Harry Reser. *Tommy Dorsey & His Orchestra* recorded it in 1935. In the many decades since, it has been recorded by Bing Crosby, *The Andrews Sisters*, Frank Sinatra, *The Four Seasons*, *The Carpenters*, Fred Astaire, Burl Ives Mariah Carey, James Taylor, Michael Bublé, and Bruce Springsteen.

Heat Wave & Hot Tunes: "Let It Snow!"/Frankie & "The Christmas Waltz"

Two musically gifted Jews who teamed up in Hollywood in the 1940s created the Christmas standard entitled "Let It Snow!" Several years after crafting that tune, they would create "The Christmas Waltz." The partners who created two popular Christmas tunes were composer Jule Styne and lyricist Sammy Cahn, both of whom came from humble beginnings to public glory.

Jule Styne was born Julius Stein in London, England just a few days after Christmas Day, on December 31, 1905. His family moved to America in 1912. As a child, he discovered an extraordinary musical talent. The Internet Music Database reveals that he "studied at the Chicago College of Music at the age of eight." Biography.php states, "Young Julius showed such a talent for the piano that he had performed with the Chicago, St. Louis, and Detroit Symphonies by age 10." According to the Internet Music Database, a Chicago College of Music teacher told a 13-year-old Styne that "his hands were too small and he would never make it as a concert pianist." Whether concert pianist or not, he certainly made it as a musician, proving that teachers are not always successful prophets.

The gifted Styne worked with jazz bands in the Roaring Twenties and acted as vocal coach to entertainment luminaries Shirley Temple and Alice Faye in the 1930s. He was nominated for seven Tony Awards and won two. He worked with jazz legends Ben Pollack, Benny Goodman, and Glenn Miller.

For the 1964 Broadway musical *Funny Girl* that starred Barbra Streisand,

Styne composed the music of "People," the lyrics of which were written by Bob Merrill. Styne said, "I think the greatest woman singer of my time is Barbra Streisand. I'll never live to hear anyone else who has so much. I love that voice." Streisand said of Styne, "He gave me that song ["People"] to sing and it rang chords all over the world. I may never stop singing it, appreciating it and loving the man who wrote it."

Besides collaborating with Cahn, Styne partnered in songwriting with Betty Comden, Adolph Green, Stephen Sondheim, and Bob Merrill.

In 1972, the Songwriters Hall of Fame elected Styne to its illustrious roster. He received a similar honor from the Theatre Hall of Fame in 1981 while 1990 saw him become a Kennedy Center Honoree. He has been praised by some of the biggest names in showbiz. Frank Sinatra said, "There's only one Jule Styne, and I love him." According to Canadian writer and cultural commentator Mark Steyn, he met Jule Styne and "noticed he wore a gold identity bracelet." Styne displayed an inscription on the inside of the bracelet: "To Jule, who knew me when, Frankie." Steyn writes that the bracelet was "a gift from Sinatra delivered to a bleary Styne by a courier from Cartier's the morning after the singer's spectacular solo debut at the Paramount Theatre in 1942."

Steyn died of heart failure in 1994, at the age of 88, in New York City.

Sammy Cahn was born Samuel Cohen in New York City in 1913. Songwriters Hall of Fame reports, "Early on, he learned to play the violin, and from the time he was fourteen he played in local Bar Mitzvah bands." At the age of 16, he wrote the song, "Like Niagara Falls, I'm Falling for You." Cahn was a violinist for vaudeville orchestras and authored nightclub scores. Along with Saul Chaplin, he put together a dance band. An article by Steve Cohen relates that Samuel Cohen altered his surname because he thought Cohen "sounded too Jewish" and believed "Cahn" might be "considered a gentile German name by potential employers." It should be remembered that he obscured his Hebraic background only for employment purposes since, as Cohen relates, "Sammy certainly was Jewish. His conversation was sprinkled with Yiddish, and he gave his children [Jewish] religious education."

In 1937, Cahn and Chaplin worked a Yiddish song entitled "Bei Mir Bistu Shein" into a mostly-English modern song. Oddly, Cahn and Chaplin believed "Bei Mir Bist Du Shein" was an old Yiddish folk song but it was not. In fact, it had been written by composer Sholom Second and lyricist Jacob Jacobs for a 1932 Yiddish language musical entitled *I Would If I Could* in English and *Men Ken Lebn Nor Men Lost Nisht* in Yiddish. Cahn and Chaplin took the title from Yiddish to the German "Bei Mir Bist Du Schon" and a then-unknown group called the Andrews Sisters recorded it. The Andrews Sisters sing "Bei Mir Bist Du Shein means let me explain/Bei Mir Bist Du Shein means you're grand/Bei Mir Bist Du Shein —again I'll explain/ It means that you're the fairest in the land." The Songwriters Hall of Fame notes, "The Andrews Sisters had a huge hit with the song, and Cahn and Chaplin were on their way."

Both Cahn and Chaplin moved to Hollywood in 1940. The collaborated on songs for Columbia Pictures for a couple of years. After a couple of years, each went his own professional way.

Cahn met Styne and the two began collaborating, Cahn usually doing the lyrics and Styne writing the musical notes. The prolific pair worked together on songs, crafting such winners as "I've Heard that Song Before" (1942), "Saturday Night is the Loneliest Night of the week" (1944), and "Time After Time" (1947).

"I've Heard that Song Before" was in the 1942 motion picture *Youth on Parade* in which it was "officially" sung by Martha O'Driscoll but dubbed by Margaret Whiting. The tune was nominated for the Academy Award for Best Original Song in 1942 but lost out to Irving Berlin's inimitable "White Christmas." "I've Heard that Song Before" is heard in the 1986 Woody Allen film *Hannah and Her Sisters*.

Collaborating with James Van Heusen, Cahn helped write "All the Way" for the Frank Sinatra movie, *The Joker Is Wild*. Altogether, Sinatra recorded 89 Cahn songs. In 1974, Cahn performed a one-man show on Broadway entitled *Words and Music*. Cahn had a hand in no less than four songs that won Academy Awards: "Three Coins in the Fountain," High Hopes," "All the

Way," and "Call Me Irresponsible." As of this writing, he holds the record for most Academy Awards for Song. He has a star on the Hollywood Walk of fame. In 1972, he went into the American Songwriters Hall of Fame. He died in 1993. On his gravestone is the wry line, "Sleep with a Smile."

The writing of "Let It Snow!" was inspired by a 1945 heat wave that caused Cahn and Styne — along with much of the population! — discomfort. Both were likely perspiring and run down when Cahn suggested to Styne, "Why don't we go down to the beach and cool off?"

"Why don't we stay here and write a winter song?" Styne replied.

Cahn took the suggestion to heart and scurried to his typewriter. He let his imagination transport him to a day when the weather was the reverse of what it was on that day. Cahn wrote the lyrics, Styne created the tune, and a Christmas classic was made.

The song was soon recorded by Vaughn Monroe and has since been recorded by such top singers as Patsy Cline, Garth Brooks, Herb Alpert, Carly Simon, Harry Connick, Jr., Chris Isaak, and Dean Martin — with Martin's version one of the most famous and popular. As the Songfacts website notes, "It fit his image as a swinging member of the Rat Pack without a care in the world."

Although "Let It Snow!" is considered a Christmas standard, the lyrics make no actual mention of the holiday. But it has become strongly associated with Christmas. The longing of its writers is evident in the repeated, "Let it snow, let it snow, let it snow." The lyrics display a kind of coziness and comfort in the home with its reference to popcorn popping. The song brings into its scene the idea of the narrator and a loved one kissing and that affection leads to a warmth that neatly contrasts with the frigidity of winter weather.

The prolific pair would also co-author a song with "Christmas" in its title. In 1954, Frank Sinatra contacted Styne to tell the songwriter that the Chairman of the Board wanted a new Christmas song. Styne relayed Sinatra's desire to Cahn who thought it would be special to create a Christmas song that was also a waltz. Cahn requested that Styne play a waltz on which was already working. Cahn wrote the lyrics making it relevant to Christmas.

Part of what distinguishes waltz pieces is that they are written in "three-quarter time" — a characteristic referred to in the lyrics of the song itself. "The Christmas Waltz" was brought into being. Since Frank Sinatra first recorded "The Christmas Waltz," it has been recorded by a wide variety of singers including Harry Connick, Jr., Doris Day, Tony Bennett, Natalie Cole, Bing Crosby, Peggy Lee, and Johnny Mathis. It also been recorded by musical groups like *The Carpenters* and *The Osmonds*.

The 1945 Heat Wave Births "The Christmas Song (AKA Chestnuts Roasting On An Open Fire)"

Oh, man! The sweltering heat of the summer of 1945 in July was really getting to Bob Wells. The accomplished songwriter desperately tried to fantasize himself out of the hot weather. He wrote a few notes on a pad about the weather as he imagined it to be: "Chestnuts roasting on an open fire/Jack Frost nipping at your nose/Yuletide carols being sung by a choir/And folks dressed up like Eskimos."

Wells' friend and frequent musical collaborator Mel Tormé showed up at the Wells house for a writing session. Tormé let himself in the door and called, "Bob?!" But Wells did not answer. Tormé walked over to the piano. He saw the notepad with the quoted four lines. Then Wells walked into the room, dressed in a t-shirt and shorts. Tormé asked about the little poem.

"It's so damn hot today, I thought I'd write something to cool myself off," Wells replied. "All I could think of was Christmas and cold weather." According to Performingsongwriter.com, "The 'chestnuts roasting on an open fire' image was a memory from Wells' childhood in Boston, when there'd be vendors on street corners at Christmas, serving up paper cones full of roasted chestnuts."

Tormé was immediately impressed and remarked, "I think you might have something here." Then he plopped down on the seat before the piano. A melody appropriate to the lines suggested itself to Tormé and Wells took up a pen and the notepad.

"The Christmas Song" was complete about 45 minutes later.

Thus, the hot weather of 1945 helped create at least two Christmas classics: "Let It Snow!" and "The Christmas Song."

Created in less than an hour, "The Christmas Song" is a remarkable work. The first paragraph instantly conjures up the sense of cold and snow along with the cheerful exuberance of "Yuletide carols being sung by a choir." The traditional Christmas meal of turkey, the beauty of the mistletoe, lead appropriately to youngsters so excited they find it hard to sleep. The following paragraph about Santa and toys rings in the love and generosity of Christmas and the lines about "kids" who are really kids and "kids" who might be elderly brings up the way Christmas possesses a special appeal for children even as it speaks to the child inside every adult. "The Christmas Song" is as merry a Christmas tune as ever has been or will be. Perhaps because the verse about the chestnuts is so beautifully evocative, the song itself is often known as "Chestnuts Roasting on an Open Fire."

And, like several other beloved Christmas songs, "The Christmas Song" was co-authored by two Jews. Bob Wells was born Robert Wells Levinson in Raymond, Washington in 1922. As a youth, he attended the University of Southern California where he majored in speech and drama. *The Independent* reported that he "wrote radio scripts before serving in the US Army Air Force during the Second World War."

The Wayback Machine records that the success of "The Christmas Song" led to "a buzz of excitement for new song material being turned out under a contract with the Burke and Van Heusen music publishing firm. One of the most important of these was 'County Fair,' which appeared in the motion picture *So Dear To My Heart* [1948], winning an Oscar nomination in the process." According to The Independent, the Wells-Tormé partnership ended in 1949. Of course, both men continued their wonderfully productive careers.

Leading producer and director Blake Edwards employed Wells for *A Shot in the Dark* (1964) and *10* (1979). A song Wells co-wrote with Henry Mancini, "It's Easy to Say," was nominated for an Academy Award.

The prolific Bob Wells authored or co-authored about 400 songs and was writer and/or producer for many television series and TV specials. Indeed, he worked as both producer and head writer for 107 hours of *The Dinah Shore Chevy Show* — and the richly talented Wells was recognized for his work by winning an Emmy for each year of that show!

Wells wrote nightclub material for such entertainment heavyweights as Shirley MacLaine, Harry Belafonte, Ann Margaret, Peggy Lee, Andy Williams, Leslie Uggams, and Nat King Cole. He also wrote nightclub music for his wife, Lisa Kirk.

Wells died in Santa Monica, California in 1998.

Chicago, Illinois was the birthplace of Mel Tormé, who came into the world in 1925. His Jewish parents had immigrated to the United States from Russia. A true musical prodigy, he was singing professionally by the age of four! He was still a teenager when beating the drums in Chico Marx's band. His wonderfully smooth tenor voice garnered him the admiring nickname "The Velvet Fog."

In 1940, the Velvet Fog formed his own jazz band that he christened the *Mel-Tones*. The band released "What Is This Thing Called Love?" The song was an immediate hit and has become a standard jazz tune. Ethel Waters said Tormé was "the only white man who sings with the soul of a black man." (Interestingly, that black woman had no trouble seeing a Jewish man as "white" although some people do not regard any Jew as white.) Bing Crosby praised him as "the most fantastic musical performer I've ever seen."

The multi-talented Tormé also acted and wrote. One of his best-known books was *The Other Side of the Rainbow*, a recollection of his experiences working with Judy Garland on her short-lived variety series.

The Big Band Jazz Hall of Fame inducted Tormé into it in 1990. He received a Grammy Lifetime Achievement Ward in February 1999 and died later that same year from health problems related to a stroke.

Both Bob Wells and Mel Tormé contributed mightily to the entertainment industry. It is likely "The Christmas Song" is their most widely treasured contribution to American popular culture. It has been recorded by such diverse artists as Liberace, Perry Como, Bing Crosby, Christina Aguilera, Michael Bublé, Justin Bieber, and Lauren Daigle.

"The Christmas Song" is most strongly associated with the one and only Nat King Cole. Born Nathaniel Adams Coles, this brilliant musician began his career as a pianist specializing in jazz. In the 1930s, he formed the King Cole Trio. The group recorded hits like "Straighten Up and Fly Right" in 1943.

1946 saw Cole's first recording of "The Christmas Song." Writer Lou Haviland observes that this recording "helped to change the course of [Cole's] career from predominantly jazz musician and singer to sentimental standards performer." It also made Cole the first African-American performer to record a popular Christmas tune. Writing for *Time*, Wook Kim reports that Nat King Cole "did four different recordings (with his trio and as a solo performer) between 1946 and 1961." The Performingsongwriter website states that the version Cole recorded in 1961, "with his voice at its smokiest, is the one that has become the definitive holiday standard."

A multitude of artists have recorded "The Christmas Song" and will undoubtedly continue to do so but Nat King Cole will continue to be associated with the song for his definitively beautiful version of it.

I'll Be Home for Christmas: Dangers & Dreams

It was 1943 and lyricist James Kimball "Kim" Gannon wanted to write something that would express the frustration so many young American men (and some women, although females were exempt from both the draft and combat) felt about being away from their friends and families, a frustration especially acute during the holiday season. Gannon wrote a song about the yearnings of a soldier at war for home at Christmastime.

Like several other great Christmas songs, this one came about because of a collaboration between a Gentile and a Jew. Gannon was Irish-American. When he finished the above lyrics, he took them to composer Walter Kent, a Jewish-American who wrote the tune for the song.

"I'll Be Home For Christmas" was first recorded by none other than Bing Crosby, who had been the first to record "White Christmas," which he had done the previous year. The recording by Crosby, done in his trademark beautifully smooth baritone, instantly shot to the top of the record charts. In a piece for *Mother Nature Network*, Channie Kirschner reports, "It became one of the most requested songs at Crosby's many USO shows throughout World War II and remains a favorite."

In a book entitled *The Christmas Carol Reader*, William Studwell writes, "Due to its very personal yet widely appealing lyrics, and its appropriately tender yet confidently transporting melody, it has lasted many years beyond the distressing war period of separation. Long after the reunions with friends and family were over, and the uniforms hung in the back closets, the song has continued to serve as a medium for past holiday reminiscences, and for future nostalgia."

However, the song ran smack into a snag as to who could take credit for its creation. The song collection section of the Library of Congress website relates, "The label on Crosby's recording credits 'I'll Be Home for Christmas' to Kent, Gannon, and Sam "Buck" Ram. Later versions credit only Kent and Gannon." The reason for the inclusion of Ram, a songwriter, music arranger, and producer, is that he had authored and copyrighted — on December 21, 1943 — a song entitled "I'll Be Home for Christmas (Tho' Just in Memory)." Although Ram's song bore little resemblance to the tune created by Gannon and Kent, the identical title led, inevitably, to confusion.

Gannon and Kent copyrighted their version of the song on September 27, 1943. Their version was indeed the one that Crosby made famous and that has become a Christmas standard. Perry Como released a version 1946 and Frank Sinatra had a record of it out in 1957. Elvis Presley, Johnny Mathis, Connie Francis, Anita Baker, *The Carpenters*, Kelly Clarkson, Michael Buble, and Demi Lovato have also recorded "I'll Be Home for Christmas."

The song earned a place in the history of the space program! Astronauts Frank Borman and James Lovell had set a record for the longest flight in the American space program when, in December 1965, they were asked by

NASA communications people if they wished any song sent up to them. They asked for "I'll Be Home for Christmas."

As might be guessed, Kim Gannon and Walter Kent were well-equipped to create a Christmas standard.

Gannon was born in 1900 in New York City to an Irish-American family. As a young man, he was educated at St. Lawrence University at which he earned a BS and then at Albany Law School from which he received an LL.B. In 1934, he was admitted to the New York Bar.

In 1939, he decided to try his hand at songwriting — and a good decision it was for he soon enjoyed success. That very year of 1939 saw the publication of his first song, "For Tonight." He was soon writing and composing songs for the motion picture industry. Among his best known film productions were the title song for the motion picture *Always In My Heart* (1942). He began writing for the theater and, together with frequent collaborator Walter Kent, produced the score for the 1951 Broadway play, *Seventeen*. Gannon often collaborated on songs, working with Kent and with others such as Mabel Wayne, J. Fred Coots, and Max Steiner.

Walter Kent was born Walter Kaufman in 1911 in New York City. In an "Artist Biography" for the all music website, Steve Huey writes that Kent "attended CCNY and studied music at the prestigious Julliard School." Like Gannon, Kent pursued a career outside the entertainment field. Kent was a practicing architect. He also conducted an orchestra that was heard over the radio airwaves and in theaters. In 1943, he began making his home in Hollywood where he worked in architecture as well as music. His popular song compositions include "Puleeze, Mr. Hemingway," "Apple Blossoms and Chapel Bells," "I Cross My Fingers," and "Never A Day Goes By."

Kent wrote the music for "Bluebirds Over the White Cliffs of Dover," the lyrics of which Nat Burton had penned. Burton wrote the song to express the feelings of British people suffering an onslaught of bombing in World War II: "There'll be bluebirds over/The white cliffs of Dover/Tomorrow, just you wait and see/There'll be love and laughter and peace ever after." The song spoke powerfully to the yearnings of the British who were, as Dick Vosburgh observed in an article for *The Independent*, untroubled by the fact that Burton was "unaware that the bluebird is not indigenous to Britain."

At the time he penned the tune, Kent had never visited those awesomely gorgeous chalk cliffs. When he finally visited the Dover cliffs in 1989, he commented, "It's how I imagined they would be all those years ago." A *Los Angeles Times* article reported, "In Dover, he participated in planning a tourist center, to further commemorate the area where millions faced the Nazi onslaught. It was envisioned as the first of several heritage centers in Britain, and Kent donated an original manuscript of his song."

Kent resided in Woodland Hills, a suburb of Los Angeles, California, at the time of his death in 1994. Co-author Gannon had shrugged off the mortal coil two decades previously, in 1974.

Tinkle — Oops! — Silver Bells

Jay Livingston and Ray Evans were both born in 1915 to Jewish families in small town America. Livingston's birthplace was McDonald, Pennsylvania and his parents were Maurice and Rose Livingston. His father sold shoes. Attracted to music from an early age, Jay learned piano as a child. By his teen years, he worked as a musician at parties and nightspots.

Ray Evans was born in Salamanca, New York to Philip and Frances Evans. His father was a scrap dealer. Ray studied clarinet and saxophone in high school, also organizing a dance band at the school.

Livingston and Evans met at the University of Pennsylvania and started a musical partnership that lasted six decades. When the pair graduated from college, they headed for New York City. Their first hit was the 1941 tune "G-Bye Now."

World War II interrupted their partnership. Livingston was drafted. While Livingston was in the Army, Evans worked as a bookkeeper at a Long Island aircraft plant.

Livingston and Evans revived their collaboration in 1944. Together they co-wrote hundreds of songs. Their song, "Buttons and Bows," written for the

1948 Bob Hope comedy-western, *The Paleface*, garnered an Academy Award for Best Song in a Motion Picture. They also authored a song they titled "Prima Donna." Evans' wife, Wyn, did not like the sound of the title. She was an art lover and suggested they name the song after Leonardo Da Vinci's most famous painting. Evans relayed the suggestion to Livingston and the title was changed to "Mona Lisa." Under that title, it played in the 1950 film *Captain Carey, U. S. A.* and won the two of them another Best Song Oscar. It was also recorded by Nat King Cole and became one of his greatest hits.

However, according to a Teresa Coppens article, the careers of the dynamic duo were in something of a lull when Paramount Pictures assigned them to write a Christmas song for the 1951 Bob Hope vehicle, *The Lemon Drop Kid*. Coppens writes that the pair were "very reluctant to write a Christmas song as new ones" had not recently been hits. What's more, "Their uncertainty about taking on such a project also stemmed from the fact that their contracts were coming due and they had not written a big hit in a while." Nevertheless, they worked at it — and inspiration struck. They titled the song, "Tinkle Bells." A happy Livingston told his wife about the song and she was appalled at the title. "Are you out of your mind?" she asked her husband. "Do you know what 'tinkle' means?" She explained to him that it was a common slang term for urination.

Livingston relayed this to Evans and they retitled the number "Silver Bells " — making it the second song by the pair to be re-titled because of the objection of a wife.

Why did they center their Christmas song around bells? There are conflicting stories about the reason for this. Livingston told a journalist that inspiration was drawn from the bells rung by "Santa Clauses and Salvation Army solicitors on New York City street corners." Another journalist was told by Evans that "the song was inspired by a bell that sat on an office desk" he and Livingston shared.

In *The Lemon Drop Kid*, Bob Hope and Marilyn Maxwell sang "Silver Bells." The following year, in 1952, Bing Crosby and Carol Richards recorded the tune. Bob Hope incorporated the song into his Christmas specials. The popularity of the song led Livingston to wryly call it "our annuity."

After the success of "Silver Bells," the Livingston and Evans continued their partnership, writing many more tunes including another Academy Award winner, "Que Sera Sera," that Doris Day sang in Alfred Hitchcock's 1956 *The Man Who Knew Too Much*. Films that boasted songs by the dynamite duo included *Aaron Slick from Punkins Crick* (1952), *Mr. Roberts* (1954), Alfred Hitchcock's *Vertigo* (1957), and *Wait Until Dark* (1967). They also wrote theme music for such popular TV programs as *Bonanza* and *Mr. Ed*. Indeed, it is Livingston's voice that sings the jaunty tune that begins, "A horse is a horse/Of course, of course."

The partnership was ended by Jay Livingston's death in 2001 at the age of 86. Ray Evans passed away in 2007 when he was 92.

It's The Most Wonderful Time of the Year

Born in New York City in 1916, the man who would become known as musician, songwriter, and composer George Wylie was originally named Bernard Weissman. He started what would be a smashingly successful musical career as a pianist and arranger in 1933. He was a conductor by 1944. He played piano in clubs in New York's Catskill Mountains.

In 1946, he moved to Los Angeles, California where he authored music for motion pictures and television programs. The respected songwriter's material was sung by such luminaries as Kate Smith. He worked as a choral conductor for the *Serenade to America* and *Alan Young Show* radio programs. He conducted and arranged for several performers including America's sweetheart, Doris Day. Aside from the song that is the subject of this section, Wylie may be best known as the co-writer, with Sherwood Schwartz, of the theme music for the wacky and wildly popular 1960s sitcom *Gilligan's Island* (1964-1967). Wylie was also musical director for *The Flip Wilson Show* (1960-1970) and wrote most of the music for *The Andy Williams Show*. He made a contribution to Christmas by being music director for the special,

John Denver and the Muppets — A Christmas Together. He contributed music to the 1993 Michael Douglas movie *Falling Down*. The busy Wylie served on the Board of Directors of the American Society of Music Arrangers and Composers from 1979 through the early part of 2003. He could not serve to the end of that year as he died in May 2003.

Wylie once wryly observed, "America doesn't want great music themes — just something it can remember."

America would remember "It's the Most Wonderful Time of the Year," a song that Wylie co-wrote with frequent collaborator Eddie Pola.

Also a New York City native, Pola had Jewish parents who immigrated to the United States from Hungary. Pola was born in 1907. He began writing songs in the 1920s. The Trot To World Music website reports, "He scored one of England's first sound films, *Harmony Heaven* (1929)." In America, he produced *The Alan Young Show* on which Wylie worked as choral conductor. Pola enjoyed a lively career as an actor, producer for both radio and TV, and songwriter. His home was in Medford, Oregon when he died in 1995.

Wylie and Pola co-wrote "The Most Wonderful Time of the Year" that was first recorded by Andy Williams in 1963 and released on *The Andy Williams Christmas Album*. However, it was not released as a single; that honor was bestowed on Williams' version of "White Christmas." The website Singing the Song in My Heart reports that in a 2005 interview, Andy Williams recalled, "George Wylie, who is a vocal director, who wrote all of the choir stuff and all of the duets and trios and things that I did with all the guests, he wrote a song just for the show — I think the second Christmas show we did — called 'The Most Wonderful Time of the Year.'"

A Christmas practice that was common in Victorian times but is no longer popular, that of telling spooky tales, is mentioned in this song. At any rate, this tune is widely beloved because it is infused with the joy of Christmas.

After that first Christmas album, Williams went on to record six more. "It's the Most Wonderful Time of the Year" was heard on each of them. SongFacts states, "The song's popularity, paired with the singer's penchant for gaudy sweaters and holiday TV specials, earned him the nickname 'Mr. Christmas.'"

As is typical of the Christmas songs discussed in this book, "It's the Most Wonderful Time of the Year" went on to be recorded by many top singers including Paul Anka, Garth Brooks, Johnny Mathis, Vince Gill, Harry Connick, Jr., and Amy Grant. It was also recorded by the band *Chicago*. In 1999, Williams and Kathy Troccoli recorded it as a duet. Williams released a slightly different version of the song for the 2003 film *Surviving Christmas*. In the 2005 interview previously mentioned, Williams said that "over 30 years" the song grew into "a big standard." The hillelontario website remarks that many people are familiar with "It's The Most Wonderful Time of the Year" from "Ellen DeGeneres' segment of '12 Days of Giveaways.'"

You're A Mean One, Mr. Grinch

Again we have an example of Jewish-Gentile collaboration making a wonderful Christmas song. In this case, it is also an example of a German-American and a Jewish-American working together to craft a Christmas song. Although there is a certain amount of special irony in one partner having German ancestry, it needs to be remembered that a German-American, General Dwight Eisenhower, prosecuted the fight against Nazi Germany, and that multitudes of German-Americans served in the American military during WWII, risking — and sometimes giving — life or limb to crush the horror of Nazism.

In the case of the humorous Christmas song, "You're A Mean One, Mr. Grinch," there is a further irony in that both the German-American lyricist for the song and the Jewish-American composer had suffered from ethnic-based bigotry.

The man who would write the lyrics of "You're A Mean One, Mr. Grinch" was born Theodor Seuss Geisel in 1904 in Springfield, Massachusetts. Both his parents had immigrated from Germany and the family encountered anti-

German feeling during World War I. However, young Theodor's childhood was, overall, a happy one.

Geisel attended Dartmouth College where he edited the school's humor magazine, using "Seuss" as a pseudonym. He graduated from Dartmouth College in 1925 and did postgraduate work at the world famous Oxford University. When he returned to America, he made his home in New York City where he worked as an illustrator and humorist for various venues including *Life* and *Vanity Fair*. According to the *Encyclopedia Britannica*, Geisel "found success in advertising, providing illustrations for a number of campaigns, Geisel was especially noted for his work on ads for Flit insect repellent. Some of his characters later appeared in his children's works."

He also worked as an illustrator on several humor books. Biblio.com reports, "In 1931, Viking Press published a set of four books full of anecdotes and jokes and illustrations by Seuss, entitled *Boners*, *More Boners*, *Still More Boners*, and *Prize Boners of 1932*." Then he decided to try his hand at writing a children's book. The finished work was rejected by almost 30 publishers. He talked with a friend who worked as an editor at Vanguard Press about the book. The upshot of the conversation was the publication in 1937 of *And to Think That I Saw It on Mulberry Street* — and the launching of the careers of one of the most beloved children's authors in the world. Geisel used the pen name Dr. Seuss and would be Dr. Seuss to the public ever after. He continued publishing books for the kiddie market including the 1940 classic *Horton Hatches the Egg*. A truly inspired work, *Horton Hatches the Egg* tells the story of a lazy bird who persuades an elephant named Horton to sit on her egg for her. The elephant sticks to the job even when confronted with terrible weather and other problems, declaring, "I meant what I said and I said what I meant; an elephant's faithful 100 percent." When the egg hatches, a gloriously unique creation possessing an elephant's head and a bird's wings comes out of it.

The four "Boners" books were collected into a single volume in 1941 entitled *A Pocket Book of Boners* which was an instant bestseller.

World War II led to a change in focus for Geisel. From 1941 to 1943 he was chief editorial cartoonist for a newspaper called PM. The German-American penned cartoons blasting the anti-Semitism of Nazi Germany and cartoons deriding isolationists. He also penned cartoons in which Japanese and Japanese-Americans were caricatured in nastily racist ways. After the war, he appeared to recognize that he had been wrong to attack Japanese in racist ways and his work often emphasized the need to overcome prejudice.

Geisel enlisted in the Army in 1943. He became commander of the Animation Department of the First Motion Picture Unit of the U.S. Army Air Forces. He worked on films designed to educate and motivate the troops. One of his best remembered accomplishments was a film series featuring a character called "Private Snafu."

When the war ended, he happily returned to authoring Dr. Seuss children's books like *Yertle the Turtle and Other Stories* and *Horton Hears a Who!* In the latter novel, the elephant named Horton is again the hero, this time not hatching an egg but protecting a mini-planet called Whoville. The novel was dedicated to Mitsuki Nakamura, a dean of Doshisha University in Japan. Geisel had visited Japan in 1953 when researching a piece for *Life* magazine. Biblioblog notes, "Although he vehemently opposed the Japanese during the war, his change of heart is illustrated in this tale and the inclusive maxim of Horton the elephant: 'A person is a person, no matter how small.'" Another Geisel children's book, *The Snitches and Other Stories*, had a strong message against racial and ethnic prejudice.

Geisel also contributed mightily to the motion picture industry. With first wife Helen Palmer Geisel, he wrote the script for a documentary entitled *Design for Death* (1947); the film won an Academy Award for Best Documentary. He wrote the script for the cartoon *Gerald McBoing-Boing* (1950) that won an Academy Award for Best Short Subject, Cartoons. In 1957, the Dr. Seuss classics, *The Cat in the Hat* and *How the Grinch Stole Christmas!* were published. The latter was made into a television cartoon in 1966, leading to the creation of the rollickingly comical song that is the reason for this section in this book.

Geisel wrote a series of books targeted to beginning readers during the

1960s, among them *One Fish Two Fish Red Fish Blue Fish* (1960), *Green Eggs and Ham* (1960), and *Fox in Socks* (1965).

In the 1970s, Geisel broadened his focus, writing books such as *The Lorax* (1971) a cautionary story about the importance of conserving the environment. A Pulitzer citation "for his contributions over nearly half a century to the education and enjoyment of America's children and their parents" was awarded to him in 1984.

The final Dr. Seuss book published during his lifetime was the 1990 *Oh the Places You'll Go!* In Biblioblog, Amy Manikowski observes that this book "is still a favorite graduation present for students from kindergarten through college."

Geisel died peacefully in his sleep in September 1991 at his La Jolla, California home. His *New York Times* obituary by Eric Pace quoted an executive at Random House, Jerry Harrison, saying, "We've lost the finest talent in the history of children's books and we'll probably never see one like him again."

The man who would compose the music for "You're A Mean One, Mr. Grinch" was born in Berlin, Germany in 1920 as Albert Marcuse. His father was a psychiatrist and his mother a champion chess player. The family resolutely hid its Jewish ancestry to avoid discrimination. Indeed, the Marcuse family were practicing Christians of the Lutheran denomination. Albert was only nine years old when his father died. Mom moved herself and Albert out of a luxurious apartment and into a smaller abode out of which she ran a cooking school.

The Marcuse family had so effectively obscured their Jewish ethnicity that young Albert was about to be inducted into Hitler Youth when he left Germany for Italy in 1937. He left, at least in part, to avoid being in Hitler Youth; while the German government believed he and his family were "Aryans," the family members knew the truth. Years later, he recalled, "I grew up in a tough neighborhood — Nazi Germany." The musically gifted youth attended a music conservatory in Rome. Then he received notice that he had been drafted into the German Army. Then, as Douglas Martin reports for *The*

New York Times, "His mother sent word to her sister in Ohio, and the sister arranged for Albert to be awarded a music scholarship to the University of Cincinnati. But then he had no legal basis for being in the United States, so an eye surgeon, Dr. Elliott B. Hague, who had close ties to the university, offered to adopt him." Thus, Hague became his surname.

During his college years in Ohio, he worked in a saloon as a pianist, becoming known in the area for his enthusiastic rendition of "Beer Barrel Polka." After graduating college, he served in the U.S. military, continuing to develop and use his musical skills by playing in the special services band of the U.S. Army. America the Salad Bowl (rather than "Melting Pot" as specific ethnicities are not melted away but flourish alongside each other even as a greater American identity is created) allowed Albert Hague to reconnect with his heritage. Martin writes, "He began to proudly identify himself as a Jew."

After leaving the military, he built a successful career as a songwriter and composer. He wrote the popular tune, "Young and Foolish" for *Plain and Fancy*, a 1955 Broadway musical with an Amish theme. "Young and Foolish" would be recorded by such top-of-the-line singers as Tony Bennett and Nancy Wilson. He contributed songs to other plays including *The Madwoman of Chaillot* and *Dance Me a Song*. His score for the 1959 musical *Redhead* earned him a Tony award. Musical collaborators included Dorothy Fields and Arnold Horwitt as well as the inimitable Geisel/Dr. Seuss. Martin reported in *The New York Times*, "Mr. Hague also worked as a teacher and coach for hundreds of young actors, including Jane Fonda, Roy Schneider and Robert Redford. His special expertise was preparing actors for the thorny process of auditioning."

Hague died in Marina del Rey, California in 2001.

Geisel and Hague were two very different people but it seems likely that the parallels in their backgrounds bestowed a special frisson to their professional relationship and played into the creating of "You're A Mean One, Mr. Grinch." Geisel wrote the wonderfully comic lyrics and Hague wrote the music. The song was made for the 1966 television cartoon version of the wonderful Dr. Seuss classic, *How the Grinch Stole Christmas*. The sprightly lyrics showcase the bountifully talented Geisel/Dr. Seuss at his creative best.

In the televised cartoon, the legendary horror icon Boris Karloff voiced the Grinch and that led many to assume he also sang the song. However, Karloff was unable to sing and the voice singing the song is that of Thurl Ravenscroft, most famous as the voice of "Tony the Tiger" in commercials for Kellogg's Frosted Flakes. Ravenscroft's "They're grrrrrreat!" made the TV audience think there must be something magical about the breakfast cereal.

Ron Howard's live action motion picture of *How the Grinch Stole Christmas* was released in 2000 and starred Jim Carrey. In that film, Carrey and rapper Busta Rhymes sing "You're a Mean One, Mr. Grinch." The song has been covered by other singers, among them RuPaul, Aimee Mann, and CeeLo Green. The delightful comedy of the song has made it a lovably eccentric Christmas classic.

Rudolph the Montgomery Ward Reindeer

In the early decades of the twentieth century, the Montgomery Ward department store hired a business to craft Christmas-themed coloring booklets. The retail giant had its store Santa Clauses give them away at Christmastime as promotional items. In 1939, Montgomery Ward executives decided it would be more economical to have such a coloring book crafted by one of its own employees.

The job was assigned to copywriter Robert "Bob" May, 34. Snopes. com notes that he was selected for this job because he "had a penchant for writing children's stories and limericks."

May was born in 1905 and raised in an affluent Jewish family; his father was a lumber merchant. However, like so many others, the May family saw its wealth to a large extent wiped out with the coming of the Great Depression. As a youth, Bob May married a woman named Evelyn. The couple moved to Chicago where he was able to get a job with the Montgomery Ward company as a copywriter for its catalogs. In a *Washington Examiner* piece, J. Mark

Powell observes, "The hours were long and the pay was low, but in those days having a job, any job, was a blessing."

When May was assigned to create the 1939 Montgomery Ward's Christmas coloring booklet, the boss told May to make the book a story revolving around an animal character. This was a reasonable suggestion since children tend to like stories about animals.

Exactly what form should this story take? May soon decided that he wanted the story to be about an underdog of some sort who overcomes his problems and triumphs. He was to some degree inspired by the classic tale of the Ugly Duckling but also by his own history.

As a child, May had been frequently teased and bullied because he was shorter and thinner than average. The teasing led to a shy personality that in turn made him even more of a target for teasing.

It is also quite possible, even likely, that he had a sense of "other-ness" as a Jew in a majority-Gentile world.

The copywriter discussed the project with his wife, Evelyn, who had also been a target for bullies as a child. She told her husband that other children often would not let her play in their games.

May pondered the question of what animal he should pick as the protagonist of his story. He recalled visiting the Chicago Lincoln Park Zoo with his daughter, 4-year-old Barbara. The child had been entranced with the deer at the zoo. Since reindeer pull the sleigh for Santa Claus, he decided, a reindeer would be appropriate for a Christmas-themed tale.

May believed a physical abnormality should be the reason for his reindeer character's "outsider" status but found it difficult to come up with an appropriate defect. Gazing through the window on an especially foggy evening, he had a "eureka" moment: "Suddenly I had it! A nose! A bright red nose that would shine through fog like a spotlight!"

What should he name this reindeer with a bright red spotlight-like nose? He toyed with naming the character "Rollo" but decided that was a bit too happy-go-lucky for a protagonist that starts out as an outcast. Perhaps "Randolph" would be appropriate? No, he thought after consideration,

"Randolph" might have a British flavor that would be inappropriate for his American audience. (It seems he wanted to give his reindeer a name that started with the same letter as its species designation, perhaps because alliteration makes a term catchy). He thought about naming his reindeer "Rudolph." Exactly why he settled on this name is unknown but there is an account that states Barbara preferred "Rudolph."

He wrote down the story of Rudolph the Red-Nosed Reindeer in a series of rhyming couplets. To be sure that it would appeal to children, he tried it out on his four-year-old daughter, Barbara, who was thrilled.

Then May went to his boss with the story. His superior was not thrilled — he feared a red nose would bring up associations with alcoholism, making it inappropriate for an inspiring Christmas story. "For gosh sakes, Bob, can't you do better than that?" the exasperated boss asked.

Convinced his story was a winner, May persuaded Denver Gillen, who worked in the Montgomery Ward art department, to draw pictures of a red-nosed reindeer. When the drawings were shown to May's superior, the boss's reservations evaporated. He told May to "put that story into finished form."

May dove into the work of crafting his ideas into a story presented as an epic poem. However, as he was working on this story, his wife died of cancer. As might be expected, he suffered a crushing grief. His boss told him he could take time off work.

But May did not want to stop working on the poem. "I needed Rudolph now more than ever," he later recalled. In August 1939, he had the story finished.

Since most people know Rudolph from the song penned by May's brother, Johnny Marks, it should be pointed out that the original, booklet version differs in significant ways from the beloved popular song. In May's story, Rudolph does not reside in the North Pole and is not one of Santa Claus's regular reindeer. He lives in a reindeer village. However, like the song's Rudolph, the original was teased for his big shiny red nose. Santa Claus is making his rounds on a night in which his vision is obscured by an unusually bad fog when he is delivering presents to the reindeer household to which

Rudolph belongs. Santa notices a glow from a room in that house and learns the glow is due to Rudolph's singularly bright nose. Santa asks Rudolph to lead the reindeer team and Rudolph obliges, leading Santa to say after the group has made its rounds, "By YOU last night's journey was actually bossed. Without you, I'm certain we'd all have been lost!"

The booklet telling the tale Rudolph the Red-Nosed Reindeer was published at Christmastime 1939. It was an immediate and rousing success. Snipes.com reports, "Montgomery Ward distributed 2.4 million copies of the booklet in 1939, and although wartime paper shortages curtailed printing for the next several years, a total of 6 million copies had been distributed by the end of 1946."

After WWII ended, there was a powerful demand for the licensing of the character but May did not hold copyright since he had created it as a Montgomery Ward employee. In fact, he was deeply in debt because, prior to his wife's death, the family had gone into debt to pay for her medical treatments.

In an act of true generosity, Montgomery Ward President Sewell Avery gave May the copyright in 1947, which meant that May could not only lift himself out of debt but enjoy financial comfort for the rest of his life. By that time, the widower had remarried a Montgomery Ward secretary, Virginia Newton, a Gentile of the Roman Catholic faith. She bore five children during the marriage.

In 1951, he quit his copywriting job to devote more time to managing Rudolph-related matters. In 1958, he returned to working for Montgomery Ward. He became a widower for a second time when Virginia died in 1971. He remarried again — to Virginia's sister. He died in 1976 and was buried in a Catholic cemetery. A cross is prominent on his headstone.

There is a peculiarity in Bob May's life that is especially relevant to his book. The five children of his marriage to Virginia grew up raised Catholic and one became a nun. Perhaps even more significantly, they reportedly did not even know of their father's Jewish ethnicity until they were grown!

Ten years after the booklet telling the story of Rudolph the Red-Nosed

Reindeer was published, May's brother-in-law, Johnny Marks re-wrote it as a song in 1948.

Johnny Marks was born to a Jewish family in Mount Vernon, a New York City suburb, in November 1909. His father, Louis Marks, was an electrical engineer and his grandfather was a prominent wholesale clothing manufacturer. Marks earned a B.A. in English from Colgate University and was Phi Beta Kappa. He also studied music at Columbia and told an interviewer in 1969 that he had been penning songs since the age of 13. He told that same interviewer that he had always wanted to be a songwriter. He got his wish and started earning his living as a songwriter in the mid-1930s. The dynamic, musically gifted man also produced radio programs and coached singers.

Soon after his country entered WWII, Marks volunteered for the service and spent four years in the Army. He wed Margaret May, Bob May's sister, in 1947. Writing for InterfaithFamily, Nate Bloom reports that Marks "felt sure the 'Rudolph' song would be a hit and he spent $25,000 to create a music publishing company so that he would own, lock-stock-and-barrel, the rights to his song." Marks took the song to various prominent singers including Bing Crosby and Dinah, all of whom passed on it. He took it to Gene Autry, widely known as the Singing Cowboy. Autry did not care for the song but his wife liked it and persuaded Autry to record it on the "B" side of a record released in 1949. It was an instant hit that topped the charts in 1949 and eventually sold 15 million copies.

Understandably pleased with his Christmas hit, this Jewish songwriter went on to make a specialty out of writing Christmas songs. He wrote a plethora of tunes for that holiday, including songs that have, like "Rudolph the Red-Nosed Reindeer," become standards. Those standards include "Rockin' Around the Christmas Tree" (1958), first recorded by Brenda Lee, and "A Holly Jolly Christmas" (1965), made famous with its first recording by Burl Ives. He also penned a sequel to "Rudolph the Red-Nosed Reindeer" entitled "Run Rudolph Run" that was recorded in 1958 by Chuck Barry as an energetic rock and roll tune.

And go down in history Rudolph has. "My reward is knowing that every year, when Christmas rolls around, Rudolph still brings happiness to millions, both young and old," Bob May once said. In 1964, an animated television special entitled *Rudolph the Red-Nosed Reindeer* was aired. It was narrated by Burl Ives and has become a standard Christmas program loved by millions and, as Snopes.com states, is the "longest running Christmas special in the history of television." Rudolph is seen in a variety of cartoons, ads, toys, and graced a 2014 United States Forever postage stamp.

It is easy to see Rudolph as metaphorically a Jew in a majority-Gentile society. One can even view the bright red nose as representing the large, hooked nose often associated with Jews. Of course, the association is, in fact, ambiguous. Many Jews have large noses, many have hooked noses (noses can be large without being hooked or hooked without being large) but those sorts of noses are common in many other ethnic groups as well. Those types of noses are common among Italians, Greeks, Arabs, Turks, some groups of Native Americans and some groups of North Africans. Indeed, it is not at all unusual to see a large and/or hooked nose among Germans, French, Swedes, Danes, English and other Western/Northern European ethnicities. At the same time, there are many Jews who have noses that have low bridges and noses that are small.

However, it must be added that the association between Jews and a particular type of nose *is* in the popular imagination. Barbara Streisand has been asked why she never had a rhinoplasty ("nose job") as so many people with that type of nose have. Keeping the nose she naturally has can be viewed as accepting and embracing her Jewish identity in the same way that keeping her obviously Jewish surname does.

Although it is certainly possible to see "Rudolph the Red-Nosed Reindeer" as metaphorically about the position of Jews, the popularity of the song is due to its appeal to *anyone* who has ever been bullied for any reason. Rudolph is the black kid in the mostly white neighborhood, the white kid in the mostly black neighborhood, the Hispanic kid in the Asian neighborhood, the Asian in the Hispanic neighborhood, etc. He is the kid who is picked on for his or her ethnicity for any possible permutation of majority/minority. But his appeal is far from limited to those persecuted for reasons of race or ethnicity. Rudolph is the hero of every child who was razzed for being too fat or too skinny, too tall or too short, nerdy or dumb, wearing shabby or odd clothing, lacking social graces, possessing buck teeth, frizzy hair, moles or warts, wearing eyeglasses, or anything else that stuck out and attracted teasing.

Another Johnny Marks Christmas classic is "Have a Holly Jolly Christmas," a song that emphasizes the friendliness that is intrinsic to Christmas and "jolly" sense that comes from that friendliness. Its references to mistletoe and kissing bring in the romance that can accompany this season and the way it can bring people in love closer together. Its first release was by *The Quinto Sisters* (1964) but the second release, by burly Burl Ives in 1965, really popularized this tune. Others who have covered it include Arthur Godfrey, Alan Jackson, Faith Hill, Michael Bublé, the *Café Accordion Orchestra*, the *Kustard Kings*, *Lady Antebellum*, and Johnny Mathis.

"Rockin' Around the Christmas Tree" was also penned by Johnny Marks. The sprightly spirit of rock and roll is brought to Christmas time with "Rockin' Around the Christmas Tree," a song that deliberately and successfully draws together the ancient traditions of Christmas and the emerging practices of mid-twentieth century America as it salutes "Everyone dancing' merrily/In the new old-fashioned way." First recorded by rock/pop/country/rockabilly star Brenda Lee, it has become a popular Christmas classic, a Christmas tune that can really get people dancing.

Then there is "Run Rudolph Run," a song that makes a reference to "Randolph," a name May considered but rejected for his hero. But Randolph makes a right fun reindeer foil for our dear Rudolph!

Santa Baby — Can Santa Be Sexy?

Santa Baby was written by Jewish songwriters Joan Javits and Philip Springer. They wrote it specifically to be sung by the first performer who recorded it, the lovely African-American singer and actress Eartha Kitt. In an article for the *Jewish World Review*, Nate Bloom writes that it "has often been called the sexiest Christmas song ever." The song was a big hit in 1953.

In an article in musicnotes.com, Philip Springer is quoted as recalling that Joan Javits handed him a single line, "Santa baby, just slip a sable under the tree, for me," and from that one lyric, he wrote the song's music "in five minutes." From the music and single line, Javits and Springer took three weeks to craft the entire song.

At the time the pair sought to publish "Santa Baby," two major musical organizations, ASCAP and BMI, were engaged in a serious conflict. Philip said he and Javits "had to create a fictional BMI songwriter who they named Tony Springer" and credited Tony Springer with the authorship of the song.

The musicnotes.com piece continues that in 1954 "the BMI publishers asked Joan to publish five different sets of lyrics for the song which ended up confusing the public. Since no one knew what lyric was the 'right one' to go with the song, 'Santa Baby' lost its holiday sparkle and wasn't played much until the end of its copyright term in 1981."

In that year, the copyright reverted to Javits and Philip. Javits sold her rights to Philip.

Philip tried to get DJs to play the tune but people seemed to think its time was past. Then, in 1988, A&M Records called Philip and asked if he would relinquish royalties for record sales if a top singer published "Santa Baby." He was told that the artist who wanted the song was Madonna and all sale proceeds would go to the Olympic Fund. He agreed to the plan and Madonna made "Santa Baby" a hit with a new generation.

Madonna's religious and ethnic background/history is relevant here. She was born to an Italian-American father and a French-Canadian-American mother, both Roman Catholic. At one point, she considered becoming a nun.

As an adult, she has studied the Kabalah, a Jewish tradition of mysticism, and follows some Jewish practices such as observing the Shabbat and holding a bar mitzvah for her son. However, she denies she is Jewish but says she identifies with "all religions" and does not feel bound to any particular faith.

"Santa Baby" got another boost when it was featured in the motion picture *Driving Miss Daisy*. The song played in a scene in which the Jewish Miss Daisy is upset that her Jewish daughter-in-law has behaved "like a Christian" by having a Christmas party.

The song is a wonderfully special Christmas song, not only because of its consciously and deliberately seductive aspect, but because it deals so frankly with the greed that Christmas often arouses. The narrator of the song seems to think it is better to receive than to give — and says so in a way that is likely to bring a smile to the listener's lips.

Do You Hear What I Hear?

Perhaps no Christmas song conveys the sheer beauty of the Christmas story more sensitively yet powerfully than "Do You Hear What I Hear?" Any listener, believer or not, is apt to feel transported to ancient Bethlehem through this song that is so rich with a sense of the sacred as it speaks of a lamb, a star, a shepherd, a king, and the (unnamed) wise men. There is a sense of ultimate equality in linking the shepherd and the king. The lyrics bring the story close in a concrete way by telling us a "child shivers in the cold." Then it draws us to a sense of reverence to this child who is brought "silver and gold." The transcendent is conveyed with its call to "pray for peace everywhere" followed by its prophecy that the Christ Child will "bring us goodness and light."

The song examined in this segment is yet another example of Gentile-Jewish collaboration. In this case, that collaboration was more intimate than in others as the two people who created it were married to each other. The lyrics of the song were penned by husband Noël Regney; it was set to music by wife Gloria Shayne Baker. Regney was of French ethnicity, born in France in 1920, and raised in the Roman Catholic faith. Baker was Jewish.

Born Leon Schliegner, Regney loved classical music and studied that subject at conservatories in various cities including Paris. Despite being a French citizen, the Nazi Army drafted him during the time his country was occupied by Germany. He reported for duty and briefly served. According to his stepdaughter, Patricia Spiegel, he intentionally led a German platoon of which he was a part toward a group of French partisans and was shot by his fellow French. His true loyalties came through again when he deserted the German Army to join French Resistance fighters.

When the war ended, he returned to the music that was his passion and worked as a musical director. Then he traveled to Manhattan to live in 1952. There he worked for early television shows in composing, arranging, and conducting. He also authored radio jingles.

His life would be forever changed when he spotted an attractive woman skillfully tickling the ivories of a piano in a hotel dining room. The woman was Gloria Shayne, who had changed her name from the "Shaine" that was her family surname. She had been born in 1923. Her father was a lawyer and her mother a college professor. The family was next door neighbors with Joseph and Rose Kennedy so it is obvious that she enjoyed all the security and material benefits of wealth throughout her childhood. Music was her passion from early on and she earned a bachelor's degree from the Boston University School of Music. She soon distinguished herself as a pianist, background vocalist, and music arranger and worked for some of the true greats of the American music scene like Irving Berlin and Stephen Sondheim.

Gloria Shayne and Noël Regney married about a month after they met. The newlyweds began co-writing songs. Among their best known tunes are "Rain Rain Go Away," made famous by Bobby Vinton and "Sweet Little Darlin,'" best known for being sung by Jo Stafford. Usually, Gloria penned lyrics and Noël composed the tune. However, that set-up was reversed with "Do You Hear What I Hear?" In that song, Noël was responsible for the words while Gloria crafted the musical notes. The song was written during the 1962 Cuban Missile Crisis, when President John F. Kennedy confronted the Soviet Union because it had placed ballistic missiles in Cuba. The song expresses the couple's concern for world peace. First to record "Do You Hear What I Hear?" was the Harry Simeone Chorale which released the recording shortly after Thanksgiving 1962. In 1963, Bing Crosby recorded it and the tune became a Christmas standard.

In 1963, Regney partnered with Soeur Sourer, called "The Singing Nun," to write the smash hit "Dominque."

The couple divorced several years after "Do You Hear What I Hear?" was "heard" by the world. Regney remarried and left a wife behind when he passed away in 2002. The second husband of Gloria Shayne Baker, William Baker, died in 2001, leaving her single at the time of her own 2008 demise.

The union of Gloria Shayne and Noël Regney was wonderfully fruitful from a musical viewpoint and "Do You Hear What I Hear?" is an invaluable contribution to Christmas.

Chapter 4
A Potpourri of Top Christmas Movies with Major Jewish Input

American Jewry is so prominently represented in the film industry that it might well be impossible to find a motion picture that *lacks* input from Jewish individuals. Thus, this chapter concerns itself only with a mere handful of notable Christmas films in which there was a major Jewish link in writing, directing, producing, and/or acting. The films selected for discussion include those that are classics and those that the author happens to find intriguing. This list does not purport to be inclusive by any means. There are many Christmas-themed motion pictures with major Jewish connections that will not be discussed. There may also be Jewish connections *within the films that are discussed* that will go unremarked here. However, it is the author's hope that the discussion here will be interesting and underline the greater point about the contributions made by America's Jews to Christmas.

Holiday Inn (1942): Introduction of "White Christmas"

We have already explored much about this movie, including its basic plot, its main characters, and how this 1945 motion picture led Irving Berlin to write the most popular Christmas song of all time, "White Christmas," that is sung in the film by the world famous Bing Crosby. Although it may not fit any precise definition of a "Christmas movie" — indeed, it could better be described as a "holiday" movie — *Holiday Inn* merits inclusion for introducing the world to the beauty of the song "White Christmas."

Jewish influence on this film did not stop with Irving Berlin; it also had a Jewish screenwriter, Elmer Rice (1892-1967), and a Jewish director, Mark Sandrich. What's more, the movie's star dancer, the incomparable Fred Astaire, had an ethnically Jewish father.

Elmer Rice was a playwright, novelist, and director as well as a screenwriter. Born Elmer Reizenstein in New York City in 1892, he graduated from law school in 1912. That legal background was on full display in the play he wrote, *On Trial*, that was first performed onstage in 1914. *On Trial* also showed that Rice possessed superb innovative powers as it was the first play to employ what was, to that point in time, the movie-only technique of flashbacks. Rice had a social conscience that came through in his play, *Street Scene* (1929), that had a slum tenement as its backdrop. *Street Scene* won the 1929 Pulitzer Prize for Drama.

During the 1930s, Rice's concerns as an American and his concerns as a Jew came to the forefront as his work tended to focus on the economic suffering of the Great Depression and the anti-Semitism of the Nazis with plays such as *We, the People* (1933). *Encyclopedia.com* reports, "During the war [WWII] he worked for the U.S. Office of Information, was active in the American Civil Liberties Union, and was president of the Dramatists' Guild." A play he wrote entitled *Dream Girl* was first put on in 1945 and a novel he wrote, *The Show Must Go On*, was published in 1949. He was a critic of Senator Joseph McCarthy during the 1950s. In 1957, he gave a series of lectures at the New York University. The lectures he presented and material he used were collected into a book, *The Living Theatre*, that was published in 1959. In 1963, he published his autobiography, *Minority Report*. He continued writing until he died of a heart attack in 1967.

Born in 1900 as Mark Goldstein, director and writer Mark Sandrich was known for such fine films as *Shall We Dance* (1937) and *Melody Cruise* (1933) as well as *Holiday Inn*. He directed no less than five of the nine films starring the incomparable Fred Astaire-Ginger Rogers dancing duo including the 1935 musical comedy *Top Hat*, featuring a plethora of Irving Berlin songs. Indeed, *Top Hat* was the most commercially successful of all Astaire-Rogers vehicles and is its most famous. *Top Hat* also introduced the public to the classic Berlin songs "Top Hat, White Tie and Tails" and "Cheek to Cheek."

From 1943 to 1944, Sandrich served as President of the Screen Directors Guild. Sadly, the life of this talented man was cut tragically short at the age of only forty-four years old when he died of a heart attack. At the time of Sandrich's death, he had been directing *Blue Skies* (1946) which, like *Holiday Inn*, was billed as an "Irving Berlin" musical; it was completed by director Stuart Heisler but some of Sandrich's footage is believed to be in the completed film.

Fred Astaire (1899-1987) may well be the best-known movie dancer of all time. A truly gifted performer, Astaire also distinguished himself as an actor, singer, and choreographer. He was born Frederick Austerlitz in Omaha, Nebraska. His father, Frederic "Fritz" Austerlitz, had been born in Austria to Jewish parents who had converted to Roman Catholicism; his mother, Johanna "Ann" née Geilus, was born to German emigrants of the Lutheran faith. Fritz worked at the Storz Brewing Company.

Early in the childhoods of both daughter Adele and son Fred, Ann saw show business talents in her children that she strongly encouraged. Fred was attracted to musical instruments and learned to play the accordion, piano, and clarinet in his childhood.

In 1905, the Austerlitz family suffered a major blow when Fritz unexpectedly lost his job. Bereft of the income of its breadwinner, the family headed to New York City in hopes that the talented Austerlitz kids could launch successful entertainment careers in the Big Apple. While Adele and Fred started training at a performing arts school, their mother suggested changing their name to "Astaire" because their birth name would remind people of the Battle of Austerlitz. Needless to say, that suggestion became a reality.

Fred and Adele debuted an act entitled "Juvenile Artists Presenting an Electric Musical Toe-Dancing Novelty." A newspaper lauded the pair as "the greatest child act in vaudeville." However, after the siblings had been performing for a while, the family decided the kids should take a break from show business to avoid trouble with child labor laws.

1912 saw a religious change for Fred as the child, then only 13 years of age, converted to the Episcopalian denomination. A lifelong Christian, Fred Astaire does not appear to have ever been attracted to the Jewish faith observed by ancestors on his paternal side.

After a two-year hiatus, the Astaire kids returned to show business. In 1917, the Astaires were performing on Broadway. The Roaring Twenties saw Adele and Fred making the stage rounds on Broadway and across the pond in London, England.

The brother-and-sister act ended in 1932 when Adele wed Lord Charles Cavendish and left the stage for duties as an aristocratic homemaker.

Fred Astaire returned to America and soon headed to Hollywood where he would achieve celluloid immortality with dancing partner Ginger Rogers in such lively films as *The Gay Divorcee* (1934), *Top Hat* (1935), *Swing Time* (1936), and *Carefree* (1938). The dancing duo achieved major stardom with all that entails in fabulous sums of money along with public recognition and acclaim.

At the end of the 1930s, Astaire left RKO — the studio that made the films in which he danced with Rogers — to freelance. He danced with Eleanor Powell in *Broadway Melody of 1940*. Then Astaire played opposite Bing Crosby in *Holiday Inn* and *Blue Skies* (1946). He also starred in films opposite Rita Hayworth, *You'll Never Get Rich* (1941) and *You Were Never Lovelier* (1942).

During the production of *Blue Skies*, Fred Astaire announced that he was retiring from films. In 1947, he founded Fred Astaire Dance Studios.

However, that "retirement" turned out to be a brief break. He returned to motion pictures with *Easter Parade* (1948) in which he played alongside such top stars as Judy Garland and Peter Lawford. Then he got back together with Ginger Rogers for *The Barkleys of Broadway* (1949). A series of successful musicals followed in which Fred Astaire's extraordinary dancing skills provided eye-catching highlights.

In the late 1950s and early 1960s, Astaire appeared on highly rated TV specials that prominently featured his dancing. *An Evening with Fred Astaire*, first aired in 1958, won no less than nine Emmy Awards. Astaire also branched out by playing Julian Osborne, a character who did not spend any film time dancing, in the science fiction drama *On The Beach* (1959). He played other non-dancing parts in both film and TV in the late 1950s and throughout the decade of the 1960s. However, his dancing skills were still lustrous as seen in the musical *Finian's Rainbow* (1968). He played both dancing and non-dancing roles throughout the 1970s. In his final TV appearance, he played multiple roles in the 1970s made-for-TV Christmas show, *The Man in the Santa Claus Suit*. His final motion picture role was in the 1981 horror flick *Ghost Story*. In 1987, he died of pneumonia.

Christmas Holiday (1944): From Darkness To Light

Christmas Holiday is a film noir and, as is typical of that genre, this black and white movie is filled with dark visuals, sleazy characters, and immoral, even criminal, actions. The title of the motion picture, together with its setting at Christmastime, juxtaposes the joy of Christmas with the film's nasty noir elements.

Our story opens with a group of military men assembled in rows as they are commissioned as officers. Then handsome Lieutenant Charlie Mason (Dean Harens) returns with other fellows to barracks. A Christmas tree standing tall and hung with the typical decorations tells the audience what time of the year this is. Chatting with a buddy, Charlie cheerfully shows off the wedding ring he has bought for his dear Mona and enthusiastically talks about the planned trip to San Francisco where he and Mona will marry the day after Christmas.

An older officer comes over to hand Charlie a letter. It is not good news: the woman he is about to marry informs him she has just married someone else. A clearly devastated Charlie hands the epistle to Lieutenant Tyler (David Bruce). Hoping to raise the spirits of the crushed man, Tyler invites Charlie to accompany Tyler on his planned trip to New York. Nothing doing. Charlie will head for San Francisco anyway. He appears to want to confront the woman who jilted him.

On the way to Charlie's destination, turbulent weather leads the plane to stop in New Orleans. In the hotel in which he takes refuge, people automatically wish each other a "Merry Christmas" but this is clearly no merry time for the disappointed suitor. He runs into newspaper reporter Simon Fennimore who wishes to cheer up the dejected Charlie and invites him to a nightclub, the Maison Lafitte. Lovely singer Jackie (Deanna Durbin) regales the audience, including Charlie, with her richly sweet-toned singing of *Spring Will Be A Little Late This Year*.

Simon introduces Charlie and Jackie. Then Charlie and Jackie attend a midnight Christmas Eve mass together. As the choir sings, Jackie falls into tears. After they leave the church, Jackie recounts the story of her marriage to a wastrel. Thus, most of the film's action takes place in flashback. Her real name is Abigail Minette and her husband Robert Minette (Gene Kelly) is in prison for murder. The scion of a respected family in reduced circumstances, Robert has had trouble all his life living up to his mother's expectations. He and Mother are all-too-close but Mom nevertheless welcomes Abigail into the family, hoping she will restrain Robert's worst impulses. The screenplay has moments of flashing wit as when Robert greets Mom and wife: "Good morning, Mrs. Minette. Good morning, Mrs. Minette." When mother tells Robert that there is "nothing" in the newspaper, he twinkles, "Just sixteen pages of blank paper?"

For about six months, the couple — make that triple, as Robert's Mom must be included — were quite happy. Abigail recalls, "We kept completely to ourselves, Robert, his mother, and me." However, Robert cannot resist his desire to gamble. Finding himself unable to pay his debts, he ends up murdering a bookmaker. Both mother and wife try to cover up for him. Despite their best efforts, he is caught and convicted of murder.

Mother blames Abigail: "He needed your strength.... All you gave him back was his own weakness.... You have failed!" Another nasty confrontation has Mom slapping Abigail's face and shouting, "You killed him!"

After the above events are seen in flashback, the scene cuts back to the film's present. Charlie asks what happened to Robert's mother. Abigail replies that she became a housekeeper for a wealthy family.

On Christmas Day, Charlie sees a newspaper headline revealing that Robert Minette has broken out of prison. What a Christmas present! The events that follow lead to an ending that is dark – but in which a kind of light shines through its darkness.

Christmas Holiday had both a Jewish director and a Jewish screenwriter. It also featured songs written by Jews. Director Robert Siodmak was born on August 8, 1900 in Dresden, Germany. In his youth, Siodmak worked as a film editor. In 1930, he co-directed his first film, a pseudo-documentary entitled *Menschen am Sonntag (People on Sunday)*. In 1933, as the Nazis began persecuting Jews, Siodmak, like so many of his fellow Jews, fled Germany. After departing his homeland, he lived in Paris where he continued his career as a director. In 1940, with the Nazis about to occupy France, Siodmak hightailed it to the United States.

Siodmak's early Hollywood directing career saw him making B-movies. Although these films shared the quality of being inexpensively made, they were in a variety of genres so they displayed his versatility as a filmmaker. These movies included a drama, *West Point Widow* (1941), a spy flick entitled *Fly By Night* (1942), and comedies like *My Heart Belongs to Daddy* (1942). His career star rose highly when he directed the 1943 Lon Chaney, Jr. horror classic *Son of Dracula*. He also directed the well-received noir *Phantom Lady*, the Technicolor extravaganza *Cobra Woman*, and the film noir *Christmas Holiday* that is the subject of this segment — all three of which were released in 1944.

The Spiral Staircase (1946) is often regarded as Siodmak's masterpiece. Set in New England in the early 1900s, it tells of a mentally ill man who is obsessed with perfection and murders young ladies who have deformities or disabilities. The film starred George Brent as the deranged and murderous villain and Dorothy McGuire as an intended victim, targeted because she is mute. The movie has a beautifully gothic atmosphere.

After *The Spiral Staircase* triumph, Siodmak went on to direct *The Killers* (1946), a superb and stylish adaptation of a famous Ernest Hemingway short story; *The Dark Mirror* (1946) in which police must discover which of two identical twins, both played by Olivia de Havilland, is a murderer; *Criss Cross* (1949), a thriller and gangster film; and *The File on Thelma Jordan* (1949), a film noir starring Barbara Stanwyck as a femme fatale.

Siodmak took a break from darkly serious fare with *The Crimson Pirate (1952)*, starring Burt Lancaster as a swashbuckling pirate. Filmed in lush Technicolor, the high-spirited movie is filled with spectacular action scenes and swordplay galore.

In the mid-1950s, Siodmak returned to his homeland of Germany. Rather, he returned to the part of Germany that was now West Germany, the country having been divided after its WWII defeat. In those post-de-Nazification years, he directed *Die Ratten* (1955), a drama starring Maria Schell as a homeless woman in post-war Berlin and *The Devil Strikes at Night* (1957), a film about a serial murderer. He continued directing films through the 1960s. He retired in 1970 and died of a heart attack in 1973.

Herman J. Mankiewicz, often called "Mank" or "Manky" by his friends, was born in New York City in 1897. He is best remembered as the co-screenwriter, with the legendary Orson Welles, of the 1941 classic *Citizen Kane*, a motion picture regarded by a plethora of film experts as among the best films ever made and frequently designated *the* greatest movie of all time.

Mankiewicz's Jewish parents had immigrated from Germany. Herman was a child when the Mankiewicz family left New York City to live in Wilkes-Barre, Pennsylvania for a few years before returning to the Big Apple in 1913. As a youth, Mankiewicz attended Columbia University where he earned a degree in philosophy. He worked for a time as editor of the *American Jewish Chronicle*. He served in the Marine Corps in World War I which took him overseas and to the land whence his parents had come. After the War-To-End-All-Wars ended, he left the military to work for the American Red Cross News Service in Paris. Then he covered German politics — while residing in Germany — for the *Chicago Tribune*. He also worked as publicist for legendary dancer Isadora Duncan.

In 1922, Mankiewicz returned to NYC where he began writing for publications like the *New York World* and *Vanity Fair*. He joined a group of American writers, critics, and other intellectuals who regularly met at the Algonquin Hotel and became popularly known as the "Algonquin Round Table." One of his fellow members of the Algonquin Round Table, Alexander Woollcott, said he believed Mankiewicz was the funniest man in New York. "Manky" was working at *The New Yorker* magazine when he heeded Hollywood's siren call, taking a job offer from Paramount Publix Studios. He started writing for the silent movies that were still being made. The talkies came into vogue soon after he took up residence in Hollywood and his pen wrote or co-wrote the screenplays for such films as *The Royal Family of Broadway* (1931), *Dinner at Eight* (1933), and *Pride of the Yankees* (1942). Mankiewicz spent much time with William Randolph Hearst, often being his guest during weekends in the 1930s, and that experience helped inform *Citizen Kane*. Although he enjoyed professional and financial success, Mankiewicz had a checkered personal life marred by heavy drinking, hard partying, and gambling. He died of uremic poisoning in 1953.

Jews are also linked to this film through its songs. Abigail sings Irving Berlin's "Always" privately to Robert and publicly to the nightclub audience.

The first tune Abigail warbles in the film, "Spring Will Be A Little Late This Year," had both music and lyrics written by Frank Loesser (1910-1969), a prominent Jewish-American songwriter. A website dedicated to his memory asserts that he "has been called the most versatile of Broadway composers."

As a youth, Loesser worked for a newspaper, as a process server, and in restaurants while writing songs on the side. "But Frank wanted to be a

Tin Pan Alley songwriter," Herbert Keyser states in *Geniuses of the American Musical Theatre: The Composers and Lyricists*. He and a friend managed to get hired for $100 a week to write songs plus royalties from any songs published. Keyser writes, "Over a full year's time not one song was published." Then he teamed up with William Schuman, who would eventually achieve renown as a classical composer. Loesser and Schuman were hired to write songs for performers. The pair had an arrangement by which one would write the music and the other the lyrics for a song and for the next song they would switch roles. However, most of their songs were rejected.

During the 1930s, he met an aspiring actress from Terre Haute, Indiana who had changed her name from Mary Alice Blankenbaker to the more theatrically appropriate Lynn Garland. When Frank took her home to meet his mother (his father died when Frank was a youth), she and other members of Frank's family were put off. They did not want a Gentile in their Jewish family.

Garland met Loesser when he performed in nightclubs with partner Irving Actman. Both men received an offer to write songs for Universal Studios. They readily accepted and were Hollywood bound.

However, Universal Studios was not impressed with the songs the pair churned out and they lost their jobs. Deciding to stay in California anyway, the jobless and penniless Loesser contacted Lynn Garland with a marriage proposal. She accepted and they wed in the office of a justice of the peace, with Actman serving as witness, after she got to Hollywood. His mother wrote to him to "tell him that he was a failure at music and to get a real job," Keyser reports.

Paramount hired Loesser in July 1937. He began pulling in good money and remained with Paramount until 1949. Along with co-writer Alfred Newman, Loesser authored "The Moon of Mankoora" that much of the public first heard in the Dorothy Lamour movie *Hurricane*. Loesser co-wrote with Hoagy Carmichael the songs "Small Fry," "Heart and Soul," and "Two Sleepy People." Hit followed hit as Loesser had eight songs that made the aptly named *Your Hit Parade*. Teaming up with Jule Styne, he wrote the lyrics and Styne the tunes for "I Don't Want To Walk Without You" and "Jingle, Jangle, Jingle." In 1942 he wrote the quirkily titled "Praise the Lord and Pass the Ammunition." That same year of 1942, Loesser enlisted in the Army, working with the Radio Productions Unit.

1944 saw him write both lyrics and tune for "Spring Will Be A Little Late This Year," a song both beautiful and beautifully appropriate for the film *Christmas Holiday*. During the 1940s, he was nominated for an Academy Award for three songs — "Delores," "They're Either Too Young Or Too Old," and "I Wish I Didn't Love You So." Since he was nominated without a win, he wrote to his mother that he felt like the saying "still a bridesmaid, never a bride" applied to him. In 1944, he wrote "Baby, It's Cold Outside." That song was sung by Esther Williams and Ricardo Montalban in *Neptune's Daughter* and won Loesser an Academy Award.

He did the composing for some famous Broadway musicals including *Guys and Dolls* and *How To Succeed in Business Without Really Trying*. "Today, many consider *Guys and Dolls* to be the greatest musical ever written for Broadway," Keyser comments.

Loesser enjoyed a major triumph in 1951 when he wrote the score for the Danny Kaye-Moira Shearer biographical film *Hans Christian Anderson*. That film was a major showcase for Loesser's talents with such songs as "The Inch Worm," "Thumbelina," "The King's New Clothes," "The Ugly Duckling," and "Wonderful Copenhagen."

Then he scored a Broadway hit entitled *The Most Happy Fella* that showcased songs like "Somebody, Somewhere" and, showing again Loesser's delicious sense of humor, "Ooh! My Feet!" In 1961, Loesser scored the witty and wicked spoof *How To Succeed in Business Without Really Trying*.

The 1960s appear to have been a bit traumatic for Loesser. "In the 1960s, Loesser became disenchanted with the music business," Keyser writes. "He did not understand or like rock music and was offended by young people smoking pot and demonstrating against the war in Vietnam."

In 1964, Loesser, together with Bob Fosse and Sam Spewack, worked on transforming a comedy play entitled *Once There Was A Russian* into a musical play they titled *Pleasures and Palaces*. The musical was put on but closed after only a few weeks without ever making it to Broadway. In late 1965, he began working on a musical based on the Budd Schulberg book *Señor Discretion Himself*. He worked on it until March 1968 when he just quit.

Loesser started suffering severe fatigue and pains in 1969. He died of lung cancer that year.

It's A Wonderful Life (1946): "The Greatest Gift" Indeed!

The son of a Jewish immigrant from Germany who eked out a living for his family as a traveling peddler, Philip Van Doren Stern (1900-1984) rose from humble origins to enjoy success early in life as an author and a historian specializing in writing books about Civil War events and major figures. However, he faced discouragement after writing a fictional story he titled *The Greatest Gift*. Publisher after publisher rejected it. Despite his inability to get a publisher to bring the story out, Stern himself believed in the value of the tale and was determined that it see the light of day.

Thus, in 1943 Stern printed 200 copies himself and sent them out to friends as "Christmas cards" – albeit unusually lengthy for Christmas cards! The story began: "The little town straggling up the hill was bright with colored Christmas lights. But George Pratt did not see them. He was leaning over the railing of the iron staring down moodily at the black water." He knows the water is icy cold and that he will not live long if he takes the plunge. As he leans "farther over the railing," someone says, "I wouldn't do that if I were you." George turns around to see a stout older fellow. George asks the stranger what he meant and learns that he has guessed that George is contemplating suicide. George is taken aback by the man's intuitive powers as the man appears "an unremarkable little person" except for his blue eyes. "You couldn't forget them, for they were the kindest, sharpest eyes you ever saw," the author explains. The stranger carries a "salesman's sample kit" so George surmises that he is "some sort of peddler."

The stranger tells George it is especially wrong to consider killing himself "on Christmas Eve of all times!" The fellow reminds George of his bank job, his wife Mary, and his mother. George is startled to know how this stranger would know about his job and family. Before he can ask about it, the stranger anticipates the question, saying, "Don't ask me how I know such things. It's my business to know 'em."

Still dejected, indeed, still suicidal, George challenges the stranger, who seems to know so much about George, to "give me just one good reason why I should be alive."

The stranger — who is never named — reminds George that he has a job and a family as well as his health.

George retorts that he is sick and tired of his dull work in a small town. He does not believe he has ever done anything "really useful or interesting." He often wishes he had never even been born.

The stranger informs him that his wish has been granted: George was never born. George angrily asks what is meant by that and the stranger answers: "You haven't been born. Just that."

After exclaiming, "Nuts!" George turns away from the man with his silly talk and begins walking away. The stranger runs up to him and hands him his satchel full of hairbrushes so people who do not know George — he has never been born, after all — will open their doors to him. The stranger advises George to tell people that the company that employs him is giving out hairbrushes for free. George takes the peddler's bag full of hairbrushes. When he looks up, the stranger is nowhere to be seen. He figures the fellow walked behind some bushes. He decides not to try to pursue the man as it is very cold and getting dark.

George walks back into town. He passes the house of "crotchety old Hank Biddle," with whom he had argued because George's car accidentally scraped bark from a big tree in Biddle's yard. George is puzzled to see that the tree shows no evidence of damage.

Then George reaches the bank that employs him. He is again puzzled because the building is completely dark but George is certain he left the vault light on. Then he notices a sign saying the building is "for rent or sale" and advises those interested to apply to James Silva at his real estate office. George wonders if the sign was put up by kids playing a trick. Then he notices that the building appears to be in disrepair — which should be impossible. A baffled George runs across the street where Silva's office is located. When George gets to this office, he asks what is the problem with the bank. Silva informs him that the "old bank building" has been standing empty for over a decade. He surmises that George must be a "stranger 'round these parts" since he is unfamiliar with this fact. Silva continues that a bank worker, Marty Jenkins, stole a huge amount from the bank which caused it to go broke as well as financially devastating many people in the town.

This news shocks George because, as he recalls it, Jenkins never actually worked for the bank. Rather, George and Marty Jenkins had both applied for a job at the bank and George had gotten it.

Then George asks about Marty's brother Arthur. Silva informs George that Art has been a heavy drinker since Marty absconded with the bank funds which has had a terrible effect, not only on him, but also on his wife, the former Mary Thatcher. As George recalls, Art had been George's rival for Mary's affections. Silva continues that Art and Mary live in a house "up on the hill this side of the church."

George rushes out of Silva's office. He wants to see Mary. The house by the church had been a present from his father-in-law upon his marriage. If she had wed someone else, that someone else, along with Mary herself, would have gotten it. George decides he cannot face Mary right then. Instead, he will visit his parents first to find out what they can tell him about her and her life.

A Christmas wreath hangs on the door of the familiar house. When he raises the gate latch, his parents' dog Brownie growls at him but his father holds the dog so it cannot attack. George can tell by his father's expression that Dad does not recognize George. Thus, George asks, "Is the lady of the house in?" His father indicates that she is and that he will chain the dog who can be aggressive with unfamiliar people.

When George sees his mother, she also fails to recognize him. Recalling the stranger's advice, he tells her he is from the World Cleaning Company and wants to offer her a hairbrush as a free sample, a "Christmas present from the company." Mom is happy to take the free hairbrush and invites the stranger to sit down in the parlor. George tells her he has previously visited the town and wants to know the circumstances of some people he knew such as Mary Thatcher.

As he gazes around the parlor, he is aware of something different about it but does not know exactly what has changed. Then he notices a photograph of his brother Harry. George recalls that he and Harry had their pictures taken together on Harry's sixteenth birthday. However, in this picture — of course — Harry is alone. George asks his "mother" about the boy in the photograph and the woman becomes suddenly sad. Her husband puts a comforting arm around her. Then she tells George that Harry died of drowning on the day the photograph was taken. George recalls how he and his brother had gone swimming after the visit to the photographer's studio. Harry had suffered sudden cramps and George had pulled him up out of the water. So if George had not been there ... Harry would have died. George expresses sympathy and then wishes the couple a Merry Christmas. He is stricken with shame at the thought that he has wished them a Merry Christmas right after reminding them of the death of their — only — child.

George must see Mary. He knows he will be pained when she fails to recognize him but he must see her. On his way to the house at which she resides, he passes a church and hears the choir practicing: "The organ had been practicing 'Holy Night' evening after evening until George had become thoroughly sick of it. But now the music almost tore his heart out."

He knocks at the door where he knows Mary lives. He has a hard time speaking when he sees her but manages to choke out "Merry Christmas." Trembling, he opens the satchel as he enters this home. He hands her an especially large and well-crafted brush and tells her she can have it free. Art Jenkins enters the room with "glazed" eyes and a belligerent attitude. It is clear he has been drinking. He sees sadness in Mary's eyes so he heads on his way.

Confused, George wonders if he could be having a bad dream — or if he even might be dead. When he goes down the hill, he spots the stranger still standing on the bridge. George rushes over to him and demands, "Get me out of this."

"You were granted your wish," the man answered. He elaborates that George is "the freest man on earth" since he has "no ties."

Nothing doing. George knows now that if he had not been born, the bank for which he worked would have collapsed, taking many individuals down with it; his brother would have had no one to save him from drowning; and his wife would have married a nasty drunk. "They need me here," he tells the stranger.

"You had the greatest gift of all conferred upon you — the gift of life . . . Yet you denied that gift."

George hears the church bells calling people to Christmas vespers; he desperately pleads, "I've got to get back."

Again, the odd stranger points out that George brought this on himself: it was his wish not to have been born. Still, since "it's Christmas Eve" . . . the man advises him to close his eyes and continue listening to the bells.

George follows the instructions. He feels snowdrops falling on his face and when he finally opens his eyes, the snow has obscured his vision and the unremarkable appearing but very strange stranger is nowhere in sight. He walks back to town. He wonders about what just happened: "Maybe it was all a dream, or perhaps he had been hypnotized by the smooth-flowing black water."

Jim Silva recognizes him and calls him by his name. He checks out the bank and sees that it is in good condition. He stops by his parents' house and greets his very-much-alive brother Harry. The dog is friendly to him. He is immediately recognized by both parents.

Then he goes home to his own wife and kids. He is overjoyed to see them. He kisses his wife repeatedly and is about "to tell her about his queer dream" when his fingers hit against an object — and he realizes it is the clothes brush he had given her in that world in which he had never been born.

The story possesses the power of fable. It is not hard to see in the tale the influence of Stern's upbringing as the son of a traveling peddler. In 1944, a year after Stern self-published it, *Reader's Scope* published "The Greatest Gift." Only a month after it appeared in *Reader's Scope*, it was published in *Good Housekeeping* under the title "The Man Who Was Never Born." Stern's daughter, Marguerite Stern Robinson, captured the story's appeal succinctly in an afterword to a recent edition of *The Greatest Gift*: "In this little book lies a powerful message about the significance of the lives of all of us."

"The Greatest Gift" served as the basis for a motion picture probably more strongly associated with Christmas than any other, *It's A Wonderful Life* starring Jimmy Stewart. In the book *A Short History of Film*, Wheeler Winston Dixon and Gwendolyn Audrey Foster write, "Frank Capra followed up the success of 1934's *It Happened One Night* with a string of sentimental films about small-town American values, which the director himself dubbed 'Capra corn.' *Lost Horizon* (1937), an atypical trip to exotica for the director, was a critical and financial disappointment, but in such films as *You Can't Take It with You* (1938), *Mr. Smith Goes to Washington* (1939), *Meet John Doe* (1938), and his now classic *It's a Wonderful Life* (1946), Capra extolled the virtues of the common man over the machinations of bankers and corporate interests, creating a comforting world of working-class, populist values that audiences readily identified with."

Frank Capra acquired the film rights to "The Greatest Gift" in 1945. He described his euphoria in his 1971 autobiography, *The Name Above the Title*: "It was the story I had been looking for all my life. Small town. A man, a good man, ambitious. But so busy helping others, life seems to pass him by . . . Through the eyes of a guardian angel he sees the world as it would have been had he never been born." Of course, the powers of the stranger who grants this wish are never explained in Stern's story but it is easy to see why Capra envisioned him as a guardian angel.

In the film, George Pratt is rechristened George Bailey (James Stewart) and lives in Bedford Falls, New York. It is Christmas Eve 1945 when the 38-year-old George becomes suicidal. At the beginning of the movie, various houses are seen and voiceovers let us know that people are praying for George Bailey with the most pitiful prayer from a little girl saying, "Something is wrong with Daddy. Please help him, God." These prayers reach heaven. The film shows what look like stars pulsating as they discuss the concern for George Bailey who is said by one of the supernatural entities (God? An angel?) to be sadly "discouraged." Clarence Odbody (Henry Travers), then Angel 2nd Class, is assigned to persuade George to live. If he convinces George to eschew suicide, Clarence will be promoted to Angel 1st Class and get the wings that go with that status.

To prepare for his mission, Clarence Odbody views a series of flashbacks from the major highlights of George's life. In 1919, George, then 12, lost the hearing in his left ear when he heroically saved his brother Harry from drowning. (Little George is played by Bobbie Anderson and little Harry is played by Georgie Nokes). Also, at about this time, George worked for the town pharmacist Mr. Gower (H.B. Warner). One day, distracted by his own problems, Gower puts the wrong item into someone's prescription medication. Little George catches the error and informs Gower of it. Whew! Mr. Gower is grateful to the boy who just prevented a poisoning.

In 1928, George is a personable young man who is well-liked around the town. He is also becoming aware of his own sexuality. He and two other men are chatting on the street when the sensuous young Violet Bick happens by. She is played by Gloria Grahame, an attractive and skilled actress who was famous for playing seductive "bad women" in film noir roles. "You look good," George tells her. "That's some dress you got on."

"This old thing?" she comments coquettishly. "I only wear it when I don't care how I look." Then she flips her hair flirtatiously and walks on, stopping traffic and causing a car to honk as she does so.

In another scene, George goes to a dance at which many of the town's young people are doing the Charleston and other daring dances of the era. Violet is hoping to dance with him but he favors the equally attractive, but more wholesome, Mary Hatch (Donna Reed). There is an instant and mutual attraction between George and Mary that is obvious to other people.

"Mary lights up like a firefly whenever you're around," George's mother later cheerfully informs him.

When George's father dies, George has to deal with problems with the family business, Bailey Brothers' Building and Loan. One member of the board, Henry F. Potter (Lionel Barrymore), strongly argues that the company should just be dissolved. However, the board votes to keep it going — but only if George is in charge of it. Thus, George forgoes college to run the business and gives the money he would have used as college tuition to brother Harry (Todd Karns) so he can attend college. George insists Harry promise to take over the company after earning his degree. While Harry is off at college, George works with his Uncle Billy (Thomas Mitchell) to run the family business.

It should be mentioned that Potter is to a large extent George's nemesis throughout the film. Barrymore commented that his Potter was "a mean old scrooge who cared only for money" which was in contrast to the character he played in Capra's *You Can't Take It With You* (1938) who was "a benign man who scorned materialism." Barrymore was grateful to Capra for casting the actor in "sharply contrasting characters" since "nothing pleases more an actor who wants to be well-rounded." Indeed, there is much about Potter that suggests Ebenezer Scrooge although, unlike the Dickens character, Potter is never rehabilitated from his wicked ways into the Christmas spirit of generosity.

Four years after George makes the agreement to run the business, Harry has not only earned his degree but gotten married. He is willing to keep his promise to George and assume the reins of the family business but George insists he take a job offer from his father-in-law that both believe is a better deal. George enters into matrimony with Mary. The newly hitched couple witness a run on the bank and use their $2,000 honeymoon savings to keep the business afloat.

Through Bailey Brothers' Building and Loan, George starts a housing development called Bailey Park. The housing offered is a welcome contrast to the overpriced slum housing owned by nasty old Potter.

There is a scene in which a Potter underling (Charlie Lane) informs the boss, "I'm just a little rent collector" but believes he should point out that the successful competition Potter is getting from the Bailey family is reflecting negatively on Potter. "Are the local yokels making with the David and Goliath wisecracks!" he comments.

"The Baileys have been a boil on my neck," Potter readily agrees.

George is summoned to Potter's office. "I run just about everything in the town but the Bailey Building and Loan," Potter observes. Then he makes what appears to be a very magnanimous offer: he will hire George and pay him a small fortune!

Initially tempted, George sees through the plot to recognize that Potter's goal is to close the Bailey Brothers' Building and Loan. George Just Says No to working for Potter.

A 4F because of his deaf ear, George is ineligible for the military in World War II. Harry becomes a Navy pilot and earns the Medal of Honor for protecting a troop transport by firing a Japanese aircraft down.

The town is getting ready to give Harry a hero's welcome when, on Christmas Eve 1945, Billy heads to the bank to deposit a hefty sum. Billy ribs Potter about a newspaper headline lauding Harry's achievement but accidentally wraps the envelope filled with cash into Potter's newspaper. Billy later realizes he does not know what happened to the money; Potter does, of course, but ruthlessly fails to reveal it. A bank examiner looks over the records and George is stricken at the likelihood of scandal plus criminal charges. He tries to find the funds, bitterly carps at Billy, and takes out his sense of impending doom by yelling at his wife and kids.

Would Potter give George a loan? When making this request, George offers his life insurance policy as collateral. Potter tells George he would be worth more dead than alive. Then Potter calls the cops to report George for misappropriating funds. George goes to a bar. He prays but he also gets thoroughly soused. Then he heads to a bridge, intending to end his misery through drowning.

Clarence deliberately falls into the water. George dives into the river and pulls him to shore.

Although he believes he has just saved another man's life, George expresses the wish that he had never been born. Clarence, who has already revealed to an understandably skeptical George that he is an Angel Second Class seeking the wings that will promote him to an Angel First Class, then displays to him what would have happened if George had never been born.

George sees a city named Pottersville that is glutted with sleazy bars and nightclubs. When visiting a bar, he sees a pitiful derelict abused and tossed out on the street. That poor man is Mr. Gower who served 20 years in prison for poisoning someone — George, never born, had not been there as a child to catch the error. George sees Violet hustled into a paddy wagon as she apparently sank from town flirt to town prostitute. He learns that Bailey Brothers' Building and Loan went under about a decade ago and his Uncle Billy suffered a mental collapse and has been in an insane asylum ever since. George visits Harry's grave. George had not been there to save Harry so he died during childhood. Without Harry to shoot down the Japanese plane, the troops on the ship all died. "Each man's life touches every other man's life," Clarence wisely observes. George visits Mary who has never married and, living without romantic love, seems pitifully shriveled. George yearns to see his children but, of course, since he was never born, they do not exist.

"Get me back!" George exclaims. "I want to live again!" Even if scandal and prison are his fate, George wants to live. He knows his life has been important and that the entire town needed him.

His second wish, for the reversal of his first wish, is also granted. George races home to await the arrest he believes is inevitable. As he runs home, he calls out a hearty "Merry Christmas!" even to Potter. When George arrives home, Mary and Billy tell him that the townspeople have rallied around him and donated funds to cover the missing money. Mr. Gower — a successful pharmacist, not the jailbird/derelict he would have been without George — is one of those who has helped. Violet is among the people at the Bailey house rallying around George. The sheriff tears up the arrest warrant.

A bell on the Christmas tree rings. George's daughter Zuzu announces that the ringing means an angel has just earned wings. The movie ends with love triumphant as George and his friends and family sing "Auld Lang Syne."

Oddly enough, *It's A Wonderful Life* was considered a flop when first released. It lost money at the box office; reviews were decidedly mixed. However, in the decades since its release, the film has acquired the status of a classic. Indeed, it is now such a cherished motion picture that regularly showing it on television during December has become an American Christmas tradition. In 1990, the movie was selected by the United States Congress for preservation in the National Film Registry as a film that is "culturally, historically, or aesthetically significant."

The film has many strengths but none was greater than the source material in which Philip Van Doren Stern so beautifully and completely captured the spirit of Christmas. *It's A Wonderful Life* also featured a fine script, the understanding and emotionally sensitive direction of Frank Capra, and excellent performances from all involved. Its most effective performance was probably that of Stewart who genuinely inhabited George Bailey and made the audience care deeply about his fate. In Lawrence J. Quirk's biography, *James Stewart: Behind the Scenes of a Wonderful Life*, Stewart's Bailey is described as a "decent American hero" who believes "his life has counted for nothing until an angel cues him in on all the terrible things that would have happened had he never existed." Quirk also astutely observes, "*It's a Wonderful Life* (1946) brought us Stewart, at age 38, to the apogee of his charm and charisma. The philanthropic George Bailey is one of his great, definitive roles." Quirk states that Stewart was "as affectingly human and charismatically forceful in *It's a Wonderful Life* as he ever would be."

At least one Jewish performer appeared in a character part. Playing the curmudgeonly Potter's curmudgeonly rent collector was Charlie Lane who was born Charles Levison (1905-2007). San Francisco was the city of his birth so he was one of the last survivors of the 1906 earthquake. He frequently played hard-nosed, even cranky characters and was in several Capra flicks beside *It's A Wonderful Life* including another Jimmy Stewart classic *Mr. Smith Goes To*

Washington (1939). He lived to be 102 before dying of natural causes. It was a long and productive life. Charlie Lane made good use of "The Greatest Gift."

Miracle on 34th Street (1947): The Jew-Boy and the "Shabbos Goy"

Jewish producer William Perlberg and Gentile screenwriter/director George Seaton teamed up both personally and professionally and the results of their collaboration bestowed great joy on viewing audiences. The professional alliance began in 1939 when, as a *New York Times* article related, Perlberg "was instrumental in moving Mr. Seaton out of the rut of being a gag writer." Perlberg gave the task of writing the screenplay for a serious movie, *The Song of Bernadette*, which was released in 1944 and starred Jennifer Jones, to Seaton. Again, we see how different groups can come together with a positive result as the Jewish Perlberg was involved in the making of a Roman Catholic positive motion picture like *The Song of Bernadette*.

Close friends as well as business partners, Perlberg and Seaton collaborated on a string of films including a comedy-drama, *Miracle on 34th Street*, that became a favorite Christmas movie. Based on a story by Valentine Davies, *Miracle on 34th Street* was written and directed by George Seaton and produced by William Perlberg. The film was released in 1947.

The movie opens with a man named Kris Kringle (Edmund Gwenn) shocked to learn that the Santa Claus (Percy Helton) for the annual Macy's Thanksgiving Day Parade is drunk! Kringle complains about this Santa's inebriated state to event director Doris Walker (Maureen O'Hara) and she suggests Kringle become the parade's Santa. He readily accepts the offer. Spectators are entranced by the new Santa and the Macy's department store on 34th Street hires him as their Santa Claus.

A Macy's customer (Thelma Ritter) cannot find what she wants at the store and complains to Santa who advises her that she can find the item at a nearby Gimbel's. This customer is impressed that a Macy's Santa would so want her to have her needs met that he would direct her to a competing department store. She tells the head of Macy's toy department, Julian

Shellhammer (Phillip Tonge), that she will become a regular and loyal Macy's shopper.

Doris Walker has a neighbor, Fred Gailey (John Payne), who takes Doris's daughter, little Susan Walker (Natalie Wood), to see the Macy's Santa. Walker strongly holds the opinion that it is destructive to teach children to believe in myths such as that of Santa Claus. However, after meeting this Santa, Susan starts to think that Santa Claus may actually exist. An alarmed Walker asks Kringle to straighten her daughter out and let the child know there is no real Santa so he cannot possibly be Santa. Instead, he insists to both Walker and her daughter that he really is Santa.

Walker wants to fire Kringle but this does not go over well with her boss, Macy (Henry Antrim), because Kringle has garnered positive publicity and loyal customers for Macy's. However, Macy does order a psychological evaluation of Kringle. Granville Sawyer (Porter Hall) administers that psychological evaluation. Sawyer recommends that Kringle be fired. That recommendation is taken so Kringle loses his job.

A physician at Kringle's nursing home, Dr. Pierce (James Seay), tells Walker that Kringle is harmless. Kringle moves out of the nursing home to live as a guest with Gailey. Susan shows the man she believes is Santa Claus a photograph of a house from a magazine and says she wants that as her Christmas present.

Kringle is outraged to discover that Sawyer has told someone that he, Kringle, is a mental case. Kringle hits Sawyer on the head with the latter's own umbrella. Sawyer has Kringle put in Bellevue Hospital. He is threatened with permanent commitment because of his insistence that he really is Santa Claus.

A commitment hearing is held before Judge Henry X. Harper (Gene Lockhart). District Attorney Thomas Mara (Jerome Cowan) elicits from Kringle the assertion that he is Santa Claus. Then Mara rests his case for commitment.

Gailey is Kringle's defense attorney. He argues that Kringle is not deluded because he is in fact Santa Claus. Mara requests the judge to rule that Santa does not exist but Judge Harper does not do so. Instead, he asks to hear more evidence. Macy is called to the stand and Mara asks Macy if he believes the man seeking to avoid commitment to a mental institution is Santa Claus. Clearly uncomfortable, the witness hems and haws but finally testifies, "I do!"

The slyly creative defense attorney calls a child witness to the stand — Mara's little son (Bobby Hyatt). Bailey asks the child if he believes Santa is real. The boy answers that he does. Bailey asks who told him Santa is real and he replies that his Dad did.

Changing course, Mara states that even if Santa Claus exists, can Gailey prove that Kringle is "the one and only"? This can be proven, Gailey asserts, through the United States Postal Service. Mail employees bring in bag after bag after bag filled with letters to "Santa Claus" — that were delivered to Kringle!

After seeing that display, Judge Harper dismisses the case.

A Christmas morning celebration is held but little Susan appears to doubt that Kringle is Santa because he has not delivered the house for which she asked. Kringle gives instructions for a way home that will avoid heavy traffic. As Gailey drives, Susan spots a house identical to her dream house — with a "For Sale" sign in the yard! Bailey stops the car and the excited child races into the house, shouting, "Mr. Kringle *is* Santa Claus!" Gailey tells Walker they should marry and buy this house. Walker cheerfully accepts both the marriage proposal and the housing purchase suggestion. Then he tells her that she can be sure she is marrying a fine attorney since he recently convinced a judge his client was Santa Claus! Right after this declaration, he and Walker notice a cane like one of those Kringle uses. The film ends on this whimsical note of ambiguity.

Although *Miracle* was hardly the only triumphant cinematic result of the Perlberg-Seaton relationship, it was one of the most important as this film is so beloved by audiences.

Perhaps a reason Seaton hit it off so well with Perlberg is that Seaton enjoyed a special connection with Jewish people long before he met Perlberg.

A man of Swedish ancestry, Seaton was born George Stenius (he changed his last name to Seaton as an adult because he thought it would be easier for most people to pronounce) in 1911 in South Bend, Indiana and baptized into the Roman Catholic faith. When he was still a child, the family moved to Detroit and settled into a neighborhood that was largely Jewish. The Gentile George got into the habit of performing special favors for his Hebraic pals. When his Orthodox Jewish buddies wanted to go to movie theaters on Saturdays, but were prohibited by the rules of their faith from buying tickets on the Sabbath, they handed the money to George who would buy tickets for everyone. For doing such special favors for his Jewish friends, he called himself a "Shabbos goy," which is a Hebrew term for a gentile who performs work for Jews that they are prohibited by their religious rules from performing on the Sabbath.

One day young George was, as was not unusual for him, waiting outside a synagogue for some friends. It was raining so a rabbi invited the Gentile boy to come into the temple. That rainy day had a strong influence on his life. In a book about Groucho Marx — a good friend of the adult George Seaton — Charlotte Chandler reports, "He went on to learn Hebrew and was even bar mitzvahed."

In early adulthood, he worked as an actor in stock theater companies and on radio. In 1933, he won the coveted part of the title role in *The Lone Ranger* radio series. He later asserted that he came up with the cry, "Hi-yo, Silver" because he could not whistle and the original script called for the Lone Ranger to whistle for his horse. When not acting, Seaton penned plays. An MGM executive read one of those scripts and was favorably impressed so Seaton became a contract writer for MGM in 1933. The first major film on which he worked as screenwriter was the Marx Brothers comedy, *A Day at the Races* (1937). Then he left MGM for Columbia Studios where he had his first fateful meeting with William Perlberg.

Perlberg was born to a Jewish family in 1900 in Lodz, Poland. His father was a fur manufacturer. The family moved to the United States in 1905. In the 1920s, Perlberg started working for the William Morris Agency. Then he became a personal assistant to producer Harry Cohn before becoming a producer in his own right — and joining forces with George Seaton.

As a successful man in Hollywood, Seaton wanted to join a country club. He wrangled an invitation to play golf from an exclusive country club. However, before he could join, there was something he had to ascertain. He asked an official, "Are you restricted?" The word "restricted" was code for "no Jews allowed." The man he asked answered, "Oh, yes." Seaton thanked them for the invitation but told them he had no interest in joining because "I don't believe in that kind of nonsense." He tried another country club but it was also restricted. Seaton was close friends with Bill Perlberg who belonged to the Hillcrest Country Club — a country club specifically for Jews. Seaton asked Perlberg, "It there any chance that I can get into Hillcrest?" "Sure, come on," was Perlberg's reply. He recalled, "So I put in my application and I was turned down because they didn't take gentiles." According to Groucho Marx, Hillcrest held a special meeting after Seaton's rejection — and let the "Shabbos goy" join.

Seaton worked as screenwriter on such Perlberg-produced films as *The Doctor Takes A Wife* (1940) and *This Thing Called Love* (1940). In the early 1940s, Seaton worked for 20th Century Fox. He was screenwriter for, and Perlberg the producer of, several films including *Charley's Aunt* (1941), *Ten Gentlemen from West Point* (1942) and *The Meanest Man in the World* (1943). One of their strongest collaborations was as screenwriter on Seaton's side and producer on Perlberg's for a previously mentioned classic, *The Song of Bernadette* (1943).

After achieving success as a screenwriter, Seaton turned director. During this period, the producer with whom Seaton worked was always Perlberg. They worked as a director and a producer on films including *Diamond Horseshoe* (1945), *The Shocking Miss Pilgrim* (1947), *Apartment for Peggy* (1948), and *For Heaven's Sake* (1950). The pair signed a contract in late 1950 to work for Paramount Pictures. Sometimes both worked as producers on films, among them *Rhubarb* (1951) and *Somebody Loves Me* (1952). Seaton wrote and directed, and Perlberg produced, *The Country Girl* (1954) starring

Grace Kelly and Bing Crosby. The team worked on films for MGM in the 1960s. Their final cinematic partnership was on *36 Hours*, a film Perlberg produced and Seaton directed and wrote. Released in 1964, *36 Hours* would turn out to be Perlberg's last film. He died in 1968.

Seaton announced in 1965 that the partnership had ended. Then Seaton left Hollywood to direct Broadway plays. In the late 1960s, Seaton returned to Hollywood. He enjoyed enormous success as director of the 1970 all-star drama *Airport*. He both directed and produced the 1973 *Showdown*. Although he said after making *Showdown* that he would make another film, he never did. His health began to fail, making it impractical for him to work, and cancer claimed his life in 1979.

White Christmas (1954)

Lushly filmed in color, *White Christmas* is a glorious musical that is a treat for both eyes and ears. The film's story opens in Europe during World War II on Christmas Eve in 1944. It centers on two American soldiers who have become close friends. One is Captain Bob Wallace (Bing Crosby), who is an established Broadway performer, and the other is Private Phil Davis (Danny Kaye), who hopes to make it big in show business. The buddies perform a show entitled "White Christmas" for the 151st Division.

The men in the division have been disturbed by the information that their commanding officer, Major General Thomas F. Waverly (Dean Jagger), who is very popular with the soldiers, is being relieved of command. The "White Christmas" program is winding up when he arrives to make an emotional farewell message.

Just as the performance ends, an aerial bombing raid starts! Everyone takes cover. Bob is about to be crushed by falling material when Phil bumps his superior officer out of harm's way — getting injured himself in the process.

Bob visits Phil in the hospital and thanks the private for saving his life. Is there anything Bob can do for Phil? There sure is! The private/aspiring entertainer shows Bob a duet he wrote. Phil agrees that the two of them will perform it when back in New York City.

Sure enough, after the war ends, Phil and Bob make the rounds of nightclubs and radio shows with their acts before performing on Broadway. Then they go into business together as theatrical producers. They put on a musical entitled *Playing Around*. On the day it debuts, the pair receive a letter from the man who was their mess sergeant during the war. He asks them to consider an act his two sisters are performing.

The pal-producers head to a nightclub where they watch "Sisters," an act performed by Betty (Rosemary Clooney) and Judy (Vera-Ellen). Judy entrances Phil and Bob takes an equally strong fancy to Betty. After the performance, the foursome meet.

Then the "Sisters" act heads to the Columbia Inn in Pine Tree, Vermont. However, Betty and Judy find an obstacle in the form of an irate hotel owner who believes they previously burned a rug at his hotel and even has the sheriff at the ready to slap handcuffs on them. Phil tells Betty and Judy that they can use the sleeping accommodations that he and Bob had booked aboard a train.

When Phil and Bob board, Bob is angry with Phil for making this arrangement since it means the two men must stay awake that night on the train. His anger dissipates when Betty and Judy appear. The foursome sing the tune "Snow" and the men agree to go to Pine Tree.

Although the group sang "Snow" believing that was what they would find in Pine Tree, when they get there they find nary a snow flake. In one of those wonderful coincidences so common in film, Phil and Bob learn that the owner of the inn is none other than former commanding officer General Waverly. As it happens, the inn owner is disappointed that there is no snow at Christmastime and blames the lack of it for the lack of inn guests. To attract tourists and help Waverly, Bob and Phil have the entire cast and crew of *Playing Around* come to the inn and enrich the production by having Betty and Judy do an act that is integrated into the play.

Bob learns that Waverly applied to rejoin the Army — but his application was rejected. Concerned that his old friend is depressed and suffering from a serious lack of self-worth, Bob determines to let Waverly know he is remembered and valued. Thus, Bob calls former Army pal Ed Harrison (Johnny Grant), who now hosts his own TV variety show, and persuades Harrison to issue, on television, an invitation to the men who were once under the command of General Waverly to come to the inn on Christmas Eve. Harrison suggests putting the whole thing on TV as a kind of free advertising for Bob and Phil but Bob nixes the idea. Bob does not realize that housekeeper Emma Allen (Mary Wickes) was eavesdropping on the conversation. She heard the free advertising suggestion but not Bob's rejection of it. Allen is upset because she thinks her boss is about to be depicted as a pitiful person on TV so she complains about this to Betty. This confusion leads Betty to treat Bob very coldly which leaves Bob confused and frustrated.

In the meantime, Judy has become increasingly concerned about Betty's romantic life. Judy fears that her friend and singing partner will not be open to a romantic relationship until Judy is at least engaged. Judy talks Phil into announcing their engagement. Things go awry when Betty, believing Judy about to marry, leaves on her own for a job in New York City.

Plot machinations and richly comic permutations follow until the motion picture reaches its appropriately *White Christmas* denouement.

With its lavish Technicolor cinematography, top-of-line stars, beautiful music, and heartwarming plot, *White Christmas* was an instant hit.

This Christmas-themed motion picture had a star and a director of Hebrew roots. The famous Danny Kaye was born David Daniel Kaminsky in Brooklyn, New York to Jewish immigrants from the Ukraine. His fame would become so great that the public elementary school he attended would eventually be named after him! However, his early adulthood did not have a hint of the brilliant success that would soon be his. As a young man, he held a series of jobs, working at a soda counter, clerking in an office, and being an auto insurance investigator. He was often fired from his jobs. He made a mistake at the auto insurance company that cost his employer an enormous amount of money and, unsurprisingly, led to his being summarily dismissed.

In 1933, he joined a vaudeville act called the Three Terpsichoreans. When the act opened in Utica, New York, David Daniel Kaminsky used the stage name Danny Kaye for the first time. He appeared in a comedy short in 1935 and signed for a series of comedies with Educational Pictures in 1937. The series of triumphs that would eventually render him a household name started in 1941 with the film *Lady in the Dark*. Then it was on to the 1944 comedy *Up In Arms*.

Prominent producer Samuel Goldwyn, himself Jewish, suggested Danny Kaye have an operation on his prominent nose to make Kaye look less Jewish but Kaye refused. He did allow his red hair to be dyed blonde so it would look better in Technicolor. One can surmise that this brilliant performer was quite willing to change his appearance for a better film affect — but not to obscure his heritage.

Among Kaye's better-known films are *The Secret Life of Walter Mitty* (1947), *On the Riviera* (1951), *Hans Christian Anderson* (1952), *The Court Jester* (1956), and *The Five Pennies* (1959). From 1945 to 1946, Kaye had his own radio show appropriately entitled *The Danny Kaye Show*. He appeared in England at the London Palladium in 1948. An article in *Life* magazine described the audience reaction as one of "worshipful hysteria." The Royal family laughed uproariously at Kaye's comic antics. In 1952, Kaye hosted the 24th Academy Awards. He had his own TV show, *The Danny Kaye Show*, 1963-1967, that garnered four Emmy Awards plus a Peabody Award.

"The show must go on" was a saying Kaye seemed to take to heart. He appeared in a theatrical production of the Richard Rodgers musical *Two By Two*. After tearing a ligament in his leg, he appeared onstage in a wheelchair with his leg in a cast!

Said to possess perfect pitch, Kaye excelled as a singer. On his radio show, he launched hit songs including such delightfully humorous novelty tunes as "Minnie the Moocher." *Columbia Presents Danny Kaye*, his debut album, was released in 1942 by Columbia Records. Danny Kaye hit the U.S. charts with a single entitled "I've Got A Lovely Bunch of Coconuts" that was released in

1950. The album *Danny Kaye Entertains* (1953) included tunes Kaye warbled in a theatrical production of *Lady in the Dark*.

Songs Kaye sung in musical films often became hits such as "The Ugly Duckling" and "Wonderful Copenhagen" from *Hans Christian Anderson* and several tunes he sang in *Merry Andrew* (1958).

In 1947, Kaye joined up with the Andrews Sister to record "Civilization (Bongo, Bongo, Bongo)." Danny Kaye plus the Andrews Sisters proved a successful combo and the foursome went on to record "The Woody Woodpecker Song," "Put 'em in a Box, Tie 'em with a Ribbon (And Throw 'em in the Deep Blue Sea)," and other songs. The Jewish man and the Gentile Christian trio teamed up for the Christmas tune "A Merry Christmas at Grandmother's House (Over the River and Through the Woods)." Danny Kaye and Patty Andrews recorded as a duet a cute song called "All I Want For Christmas Is My Two Front Teeth."

Throughout the 1960s and 1970s, the multi-talented Kaye conducted world famous orchestras. Zubin Mehta praised Kaye for his "very efficient conducting style" and Dimitri Mitropoulos said Kaye "gets more out of my orchestra than I have."

Kaye played a demanding dramatic role in the 1981 made-for-TV film *Skokie*. Kaye played a Holocaust survivor, a role which, as a Jew, he must have found personally deeply affecting. The movie was based on an actual case in which a group of American Nazis wanted to hold a march in Skokie, Illinois, a small town with a large Jewish population, a significant portion of which were Holocaust survivors. The Nazis were led by a man named Frank Collin (who has since renounced Nazism and reinvented himself as Frank Joseph, author of a series of books on occult and New Age topics). In playing Max Feldman, Kaye showed dramatic intensity as the character recalled living under the oppression of Nazi Germany.

Danny Kaye died of heart failure in 1987 at the age of 76.

The director of *White Christmas*, Michael Curtiz, was born Manó Kaminer to a Jewish family in Budapest, Austria-Hungary. His father was a carpenter and his mother an opera singer (isn't *that* marital combo one for the books?). Even as a child, little Manó Kaminer knew that he was called to the entertainment industry. When only eight years old, the boy constructed a little theater in the basement of the family's home. He and other children would set up a stage, complete with props and scenery, from which they acted out plays. At 19, he joined a traveling theater company as an actor. Then he got a position with a circus performing pantomimes. After that, he joined another traveling theater company that often put on classics. He traveled throughout Europe, becoming fluent in five languages.

In 1912, he directed his first feature motion picture *Today and Tomorrow*. He also acted a major part in the film. When World War I started, he went into the Hungarian military and was wounded in battle on the Russian front.

He became director of production at a leading Hungarian studio, Phoenix Films, in 1917. He directed several motion pictures during his time at Phoenix Films and was widely considered one of the country's best directors. However, in 1919, the newly communist Hungarian government nationalized the film industry and that led him to leave Hungary for Vienna. He directed a variety of motion pictures, most of them either historical spectacles or light-hearted comedies. Some of his films were set in Biblical times, among them *Sodom and Gomorrah (1922)* and *Moon of Israel* (1924), the latter about the Egyptian enslavement of the director's Hebrew ancestors and their deliverance from captivity by God through Moses.

He traveled to the United States in 1926 and changed his name to Michael Curtiz. He faced a problem because he had to learn English on the fly since he was unfamiliar with the language when he arrived on American shores. He learned the language and, by 1930, successfully directed Al Jolson in *Mammy*. Then Curtiz branched out into both horror and Technicolor with *Doctor X* (1932) and *Mystery of the Wax Museum* (1933). Neither Bette Davis or Spencer Tracy was well-known when Michael Curtiz directed them in *20,000 Years in Sing Sing* (1932) — a film that may have helped launch those performers on their way to celluloid greatness.

Curtiz enjoyed a similar honor when he directed the buccaneering *Captain Blood* (1935) starring the then little-known actor Errol Flynn alongside the then little-known actress Olivia de Havilland. *Captain Blood* was an instant hit with public and critics. Although it did not win, it was nominated for an Academy Award for Best Picture. Oddly, Curtiz was not nominated for the Academy Award for Best Director but received so many write-in votes for that honor that he came in second place!

John Garfield was another performer who made his name due to the Curtiz treatment. Garfield debuted in Curtiz's *Four Daughters* (1938) and made waves in the sequel, *Four Wives* (1939), in which Garfield co-starred with the well-established Claude Rains.

Curtiz was nominated for the Academy Award for Best Director for the James Cagney gangster flick *Angels with Dirty Faces* (1938). That same year, Curtiz was also nominated for the Academy Award for Best Director for *Four Daughters*!

In 1939, Curtiz directed *Sons of Liberty* (1939), a film that must have been especially dear to his heart since it was about the contributions of Jews to America's struggle for independence. A two reel short, only twenty minutes long, *Sons of Liberty* starred Claude Rains as Haym Salomon, a Jewish-American patriot who helped finance the American Revolution both through fundraising and his own loans. At the 1940 Academy Awards, *Sons of Liberty* won Academy Award for Best Short Subject (Two-Reel).

The 1940s saw this prodigious and talented director really coming into his own by directing a string of critically acclaimed hits: *The Sea Wolf* (1941), *Casablanca* (1942), *Yankee Doodle Dandy* (1942), and *Mildred Pierce* (1945).

Curtiz continued directing top-notch films in the 1950s, including *Young Man with a Horn* (1950), *Jim Thorpe — All-American* (1951), *The Story of Will Rogers* (1952), *King Creole* (1958) — and, of course, *White Christmas*. The final film he directed, *The Comancheros* (1952), was a John Wayne Western. On some days while *Comancheros* was being made, Curtiz was too sick from the cancer to direct so Wayne did the directing on those days. Curtiz was 75 years old when he died of cancer. He left behind a record of solid achievement that included work that spoke with special strength to his own Jewish community and *White Christmas* that paid beautiful cinematic tribute to that cherished Christian holiday.

Trading Places (1983): A Prince and a Pauper in 1980s America

Born in Chicago in 1950 to Marshall Landis, an interior designer/decorator, and Shirley Landis (née Magaziner), John Landis lived most of his childhood and adolescence in Los Angeles, California. The Landis family appears to have been troubled as Marshall Landis was charged with grand theft when John was only a baby. Dad Landis later spent time in a mental institution. After an operation, he died in 1956 so John spent most of his formative years without his father. However, his mother remarried soon after her husband's death so he had a stepfather, building contractor Walter Levine.

John nursed show business ambitions from a very young age. He would enjoy tremendous success in that field — which would also lead him into horrifying tragedy.

As a child, he viewed *The 7th Voyage of Sinbad* — and determined to become a movie director. "I had complete suspension of disbelief," he recalled as an adult. "Really, I was eight years old and it transported me. I was on that beach running from that dragon, fighting that Cyclops." His fascination with that film led him to want to make films himself. Although he often quarreled with his stepfather, Walter Levine helped his stepson construct a wooden stage from which little John often put on puppet shows for people in the neighborhood. He had a gorilla puppet of which he was especially fond; a special interest in simians continued into adulthood and was reflected in his movies.

Indeed, the fascination with apes is seen in the comedy Landis wrote, directed, and starred in when he was 21. Entitled *Schlock* (1973), Landis described the movie as "an extremely low-budget parody of extremely low-budget ape-man movies." A send-up of the monster movies Landis loved during his growing up years, *Schlock* is about a prehistoric "missing link" ape-human creature who falls in love with a blind teenaged girl. The hirsute semi-ape, semi-human also terrorizes a suburb.

During his early years in the motion picture industry, Landis often worked for Roger Corman, a director noted for low-budget flicks that often became cult films such as *Little Shop of Horrors* (1960) and *Rock 'n' Roll High School* (1979). In an introduction to a book about Corman, Landis wrote that he worked for Corman "as a crew member or stuntman, sometimes even as an actor" but does not regard himself as "an alumnus of the 'Roger Corman School of Filmmaking'" since he never directed a movie for Corman.

Landis established himself as a director through films such as *Kentucky Fried Movie* (1977) and *Animal House* (1978). Crude humor figured heavily in Landis films which tended to garner decidedly mixed reviews but made money at the box office. Together with Dan Aykroyd, he co-wrote a comedy called *The Blues Brothers* (1980). Directed by Landis, the film starred Aykroyd and John Belushi and featured musical numbers by R&B and soul music legends James Brown, Ray Charles, Cab Calloway, and Aretha Franklin. 1981 saw him write and direct *An American Werewolf in London*, a horror comedy.

The next year, 1982, was to see Landis involved in true horror. Landis learned that his friend, the brilliant and renowned Steven Spielberg, planned to make a film inspired by the original *Twilight Zone* (1959-1964) series. Landis and Spielberg agreed that they would co-produce a motion picture that followed the pattern of the TV program. Spielberg decided on an anthology of stories. Three re-created episodes that appeared in the original series: Spielberg directed "Kick the Can," about elderly people who are magically transformed back into children; another episode was "It's A Good Life" about people held prisoner by a monster-child; and a third was "Nightmare at 20,000 Feet" about a man seeing a bizarre monster on the wing of an airplane while it is in flight.

The fourth episode, which Landis directed, was the only segment that was *not* a re-creation of an original *TZ* episode. Along with directing this segment, Landis wrote the screenplay for it. He believed it was true to the spirit of Rod Serling's show. "He often used the fantasy element of his program to deal with social issues," Landis noted. "The story I made up, trying to use the magic, the idea of *Twilight Zone*, was about racism."

Indeed, it is likely that Landis is especially sensitive to the evil of racism, as Serling was, because Landis is Jewish as was Serling.

The script Landis wrote was about a bigoted white gentile man named Bill Connor. It opens with the protagonist in a bar talking with two friends. Connor goes into a tirade because he failed to get a promotion he wanted. Instead, the promotion he wanted went "to that Jew bastard." One of his friends points out that his Jewish competitor had been at the company longer than Connor so the promotion was hardly unfair but Connor remains bitter as he goes on to deride Jews, blacks, and Asians — using the usual ugly slur words so often used by bigots. Connor leaves the bar — and steps right into Nazi-occupied France. Nazi troops believe he is a Jew and chase him. Fleeing from the Nazis, he runs straight into the Jim Crow Old South in which Ku Klux Klansmen see him as a black and try to lynch him. Connor escapes from them and runs straight into Vietnam during the Vietnam War where American GIs attack him, seeing him as a Viet Cong.

In an article this author previously wrote, I pointed out that the story "had an ethical problem at its heart." That problem was appearing to equate American troops during the Vietnam War with Nazis and Ku Klux Klan. In retrospect, it is hard to avoid the conclusion that America's leaders made a horrible mistake in getting our troops involved in the Vietnam War but that does not mean that the American soldiers of all ethnic/religious/racial backgrounds who fought in that conflict were morally similar to genocidal Nazis and KKK lynchers!

Landis submitted his script to Warner Brothers executives for approval. Vice-President in charge of production Lucy Fisher and studio President Terry Semel raised objections to the screenplay. They pointed out that the protagonist was depicted so negatively that audiences might be unable to empathize with him or care about him. Thus, Landis decided to add to the script something that would show this prejudiced character overcoming his bigotry. He would run from American soldiers firing at him, and from an American helicopter pursuing him, and come upon two small Vietnamese children who appear to be war orphans. Connor's latent decency is aroused by the children's plight and he would courageously carry them away from the American attackers and across a river, saving the lives of the little ones. A Vietnamese village would be blown up in the background as the redeemed ex-racist assured the children, "I'll keep you safe, kids! I swear to God!"

Of course, the script changes meant that Landis had to employ two small children of Asian heritage. While seeking these actors, he learned that California's child labor laws could put a wrench into having children in the scene he envisioned. *TZ* casting agents Michael Fenton and Marci Liroff of Fenton-Feinberg casting informed Landis that state child labor laws made it illegal to employ children past curfew and mandated that a teacher-welfare worker be present when children worked. Much later, Liroff said she had told Landis that the scene he described seemed "kind of dangerous." Since the kids would not be speaking, Fenton further informed the director that they were extras and that meant they could not be hired through Fenton-Feinberg Casting. A journalist reported that Liroff explained, "Fenton's response was a diplomatic way to avoid involvement in a questionable venture."

The child labor laws allowed employers to seek waivers that would allow children to work past curfew — but Landis never sought such a waiver. Instead, Landis decided to just break the law by employing the children illegally and paying them out of petty cash, thus avoiding putting their names on payroll.

Two Asian children were found whose parents agreed that they could play in Landis's *Twilight Zone* segment. One was 6-year-old Renee Chen, daughter of father Mark Chen and mother Shyan-Huei Chen. Shyan-Huei was especially pleased that her child would appear in a film, saying it "would be a very fine experience" and give Renee "a lot of memories of what she had done" when she grew up. The other child was 7-year-old My-ca Le, son of Dr. Daniel Le and his wife Kim-Hoa Le. When My-ca was told of the opportunity to appear in a film, he excitedly jumped up and down, shouting, "I like it!"

The actor cast to play the bigoted Bill Connor was Vic Morrow, who had made a big splash in his youth in the juvenile delinquency drama *Blackboard Jungle* (1955). His casting as the anti-Semitic Connor is somewhat interesting since Morrow was Jewish. This, in turn, brings up a basic irony of anti-Semitism as opposed to certain other types of racism. Jews and those prejudiced against them are physically indistinguishable from each other — at least if the anti-Semite is what is usually called a "white" or "Caucasian" person. Thus, Jewish actors and actresses can play anti-Semites, including Nazis in films and plays. Similarly, Gentiles, including those who would have been considered "Aryan" in Hitler's Germany, can play Jews.

Back to the "softening" scene that was meant to evoke sympathy for Bill Connor — a scene that would play out with the most tragic real-life consequences imaginable.

In the wee hours of July 24, 1982, Landis prepared to film the scene with the children in which Connor would rescue them. Morrow went knee deep into water, carrying a child under each arm. Landis wanted to get a better shot of the helicopter so he shouted through his bullhorn at the pilot, "Lower! Lower! Lower!" His assistant repeated the order to the pilot through a walkie-talkie. Machine gunners fired and a special effects technician set off simulations of shots hitting the water. The pilot feared his craft was in trouble but could not relay this to the technician on the ground who continued detonating charges.

The helicopter went out of control and crashed. It slammed into Renee Chen and killed her. Its whirling main rotor tore off the head of Vic Morrow as well as the head and an arm of My-ca.

The mother of Renee and the father of My-ca shrieked uncontrollably in horror.

"That's a wrap!" Landis shouted over the tumult through a loudspeaker. Those standard words signaling that the filming of a scene is over seemed bizarre and incongruous to the real-life horror. He continued, "Leave your equipment where it is. Everyone go home. Please, everyone go home!"

Shyan-Huei Chen and Dr. Daniel Le did not — *could* not — immediately go home but were taken to a hospital to be treated for shock before being driven home.

Not too long after this disaster, Landis and several others were arrested in connection with it. However, prosecutors made a decision early on that puzzled some observers. Landis and the associates who had helped him hire the children would not be charged with illegally hiring children or having them work after curfew sans a legal waiver — crimes they had definitely and indisputably committed. Rather, Landis was charged with three counts of involuntary manslaughter. Some who worked under him were also charged with involuntary manslaughter.

When the *Twilight Zone* movie hit theaters, it included the segment in which Morrow played nasty Connor but did not include the part in which Connor rescues the Asian children. Rather, it appeared as Landis had originally wrote it, with the bigot's personality quite unsoftened as he receives ironic comeuppance for his prejudices.

Landis was indisputably traumatized by this horrible accident. Doctors heavily medicated the distraught director for weeks after it. At one point, Landis seemed to wonder if his career was over. "How am I ever going to be able to ask someone to take even the simplest direction?" he despairingly asked a friend shortly after the tragedy. But Landis recovered both mentally and emotionally and was soon comfortably seated in the director's chair. In the four years between the tragedy and his trial for the charges connected with it, Landis directed several projects including the Michael Jackson video *Thriller* (1983) and the motion picture that is especially relevant to this book because of its Christmastime setting, *Trading Places*.

The trial of Landis and others started on September 3, 1986. It ended with acquittals for all parties. Adult children of Morrow and parents of the dead children filed lawsuits against Landis that were settled out of court.

As of this writing, Landis continues pursuing a successful career as a director and occasionally acts and/or produces as well. Although his ethnicity is Jewish, he has stated in an interview that he is an atheist.

Trading Places is a 1983 comedy that has often been compared to the classic Mark Twain novel, *The Prince and the Pauper*. Timothy Harris and Herschel Weingold co-authored the screen play and Aaron Russo produced the film.

The reason *Trading Places* is being discussed at such length here is that it is set at Christmastime. In an article on the movie written over two decades after it came out, Gillian B. White and Bourree Lam aptly observe, "*Trading Places* isn't exactly a traditional Christmas film. There are no carolers or large family gatherings. But the trappings of a great holiday movie are there: It does, in fact, take place around the holidays, including a company Christmas party that features a drunk and disgruntled Santa Claus, and focus on themes of generosity (or lack thereof) and redemption."

The film begins with two fabulously wealthy brothers embarking upon an odd sort of experiment. Wealthy Randolph Duke (Ralph Bellamy) and Mortimer Duke (Don Ameche) live in Philadelphia were they own and operate a commodities brokerage firm called Duke & Duke Commodity Brokers. They hold opposite positions on the nature vs. nurture controversy and make a $1 bet that they think puts that controversy to the test. The brothers decide to switch the positions of two people living at extreme ends of the social hierarchy to observe how each adjusts to completely different circumstances.

The persons chosen are appropriate for this experiment. The audience first meets Billy Ray Valentine (Eddie Murphy) as a street hustler who plays at being physically disabled as he begs money from passersby. Two police officers approach him, telling him that they have heard about hustlers faking disabilities. The cops obviously suspect Valentine — wearing dark glasses to suggest he is blind and sitting on a scooter in such a way as to suggest he is legless — is one of them. Valentine gives them his usual con about being a Vietnam War veteran who was blinded and lost his legs in 'Nam. The cops remove his sunglasses and pull him up from the scooter.

Still trying to run the con, Valentine yells, "I can see! I have legs! Praise Jesus! Praise Jesus!" The police roll their eyes and look at each other in exasperation at the exposed faker.

The fellow at the "good" end of the social hierarchy is Louis Winthorpe III (Dan Ackroyd) who is engaged to Penelope Witherspoon (Kristin Holby), a grand-niece of the Duke brothers. As Valentine is walking away from the police, he quite literally runs into Winthorpe — who believes Valentine is trying to steal his briefcase. A jarring note is introduced as the audience realizes that Valentine, a street hustler and petty criminal, is innocent of this particular charge. Nevertheless, it leads to Valentine being surrounded by police with guns trained on him. It also leads Valentine to a night in jail.

The Dukes decide to have these two fellows unwittingly "trade places." The brothers enlist employee Clarence Beeks (Paul Gleason) to frame Winthorpe as a thief and illegal drug dealer; they also get Beeks to fabricate things so it appears Winthorpe has cheated on Witherspoon. Thus, Winthorpe is fired from his job at Duke & Duke and his bank accounts are frozen. He cannot get into his house — owned by the Dukes — and his former friends shun him. Believing he has been unfaithful, Penelope breaks their engagement.

The shaken and confused Winthorpe makes friends with a hooker boasting the oddly Shakespearean name Ophelia (Jamie Lee Curtis) who says she will try to help him regain his riches if — of course — he generously greases her palm if he does so.

At the same time that the Dukes are underhandedly gutting the career of Winthorpe, they act as bizarrely generous benefactors to Valentine. The brothers put up bail so Valentine can get out of the clink. Then they invite him to live in what had been Winthorpe's home. They also hire him to replace Winthorpe at what had been Winthorpe's job. The street-smart hustler possesses business acumen that he transfers to his new role as he picks up the manners and etiquette of the upper-crust.

It is supposedly a Merry Christmas for Duke & Duke as the company has a Christmas party for its employees. *Former* employee Louis Winthorpe III goes there to plant illegal dope in the desk of new employee Billy Ray Valentine. Winthorpe shows he has indeed gone "street" when he escapes by showing a gun!

Billy Ray Valentine overhears the Duke brothers discussing their bet and the odd experiment upon which they have embarked. Valentine learns that they intend to toss him back onto the streets — without giving Winthorpe back his previous privileged position. Realizing he is not the beneficiary of true largess but the subject of a callous experiment, Valentine seeks out Winthorpe and learns that the latter has survived a suicide attempt. Valentine, Ophelia, and Winthorpe's former butler Coleman (Denholm Elliott) nurse Winthorpe back to health. They also tell him of the Duke brothers bet and how he was the victim of their ensuing experiment.

Winthorpe and Valentine join forces for some plotting of their own. They learn from a TV show that Beeks possesses a secret report from the USDA on orange crop forecasts and that the Duke brothers have a plan to corner the market for frozen concentrated orange juice — a plan that Winthorpe and Valentine determine to foil.

Valentine, Winthorpe, Ophelia, and Coleman get on the train that they know Beeks is on. The conniving foursome plot to switch the report Beeks has with a fake one making an opposite prediction. Beeks learns of their plot and tries to murder them. Then Beeks is knocked out by a gorilla being transported on the train! (Once again, the lifelong fascination John Landis has had for simians is displayed in his work.) The foursome put the unconscious Beeks in a gorilla costume and push him into a cage with the real gorilla.

The forged and misleading report is delivered to the brothers Duke. Ophelia and Coleman commit their life savings to help Winthorpe and Valentine with the plot.

The climax of *Trading Places* occurs on the commodities trading floor. The Duke brothers put their entire holding into buying frozen concentrated orange juice futures contracts. Seeing their action, the other traders imitate it. Valentine and Winthorpe short sell. A broadcast of the true crop report is heard and the orange juice futures price takes a nosedive. Then Valentine and Winthorpe buy futures at a lower price and make a huge profit. The Duke brothers end up bankrupt! These nasty over-privileged American princes have been turned into paupers by their own guinea pigs. Randolph grabs at his chest and falls in an apparent shock-related heart attack while Mortimer yells about the results of their plot.

The film ends with Valentine, Winthorpe, Coleman, and Ophelia all wealthy. . . and Beeks still with the gorilla!

Semitic influence on this singularly odd but well-crafted and deeply meaningful "Christmas movie" is not limited to John Landis. Producer Aaron Russell was born in Brooklyn in 1943 to a Sephardic Jewish family that had an undergarment business. By 1968, he had taken up residence in Chicago where he opened a nightclub that was originally called the Electric Theater and then re-titled the Kinetic Playground. The rock groups that did their things at his nightclub read like a Who's Who in Rock 'n' Roll: *The Grateful Dead*, *The Who*, *Jefferson Airplane*, *Led Zeppelin*, and *Iron Butterfly*. That queen of rough sounding rock, Janis Joplin, belted it out at Russell's nightclub. Clearly musically oriented, he also acted as manager to musical acts including superstar Bette Midler and famous band *The Manhattan Transfer*.

However, he decided to get into motion pictures and produced and/or directed several films including producing *Trading Places*. Russell was also strongly interested in politics. In 1998, he ran for Nevada Governor on the Republican ticket but lost out in the Republican primary to another candidate. In 2004, he announced he was running for President of the United States, first as an Independent, and then as a Libertarian. However, he did not win the Libertarian nomination. At this time, he was already battling cancer, a battle he lost in 2007 when he died of it.

Trading Places co-writer Herschel Weingold was born in a family of Jewish ancestry in 1947 in Milwaukee, Wisconsin. He and *Trading Places* co-writer Timothy Harris also collaborated on *Kindergarten Cop* (1990), *Twins* (1988), and *Space Jam* (1996), and *Cheaper to Keep Her* (1981).

The Nightmare Before Christmas (1993)

Also called *Tim Burton's The Nightmare Before Christmas*, *The Nightmare Before Christmas* draws its witty, Gothic inspiration from a poem director Tim

Burton wrote in 1982 called "The Nightmare Before Christmas." Of course, Burton's poem took inspiration from the classic poem that is often known as "The Night Before Christmas" although it was originally titled "A Visit from St. Nicholas."

The Nightmare Before Christmas is a stop-motion animated film that was produced by Tim Burton and Denise DiNova, directed by Harry Selick, and adapted for the screen by Michael McDowell with a screenplay by Caroline Thompson.

The film opens in a fantasy creation called Halloween Town. Its residents, a varied collection of endearing goblins, ghouls, and monsters, sing a sprightly song, the chorus of which is the self-explanatory "This is Halloween!" The leader of Halloween Town is "Pumpkin King" Jack Skellington, whose name is appropriate as he is a skeleton in a suit with enormous eye-holes that apparently see like eyes.

One day Jack happens to be wandering through a forest when he finds seven trees with doors that lead to towns that, like Halloween Town, represent various holidays. He opens the door to — wouldn't you know it? — Christmas Town! Jack finds Christmas Town an exciting place of beauty and is utterly thrilled and charmed by it. He must inform Halloween Town of this wonder of wonders!

And indeed, he does. The residents of Halloween Town are also excited by the idea of Christmas Town but they have a hard time understanding it and try to relate everything Jack tells them to the familiar Halloween. They are intrigued by a Christmas Town denizen that they believe they understand, the red-coated "Sandy Claws."

Why, oh why, Jack Skellington wonders, should the residents of Christmas Town have a monopoly on the beauties of Christmas? It's not fair! He decides that Halloween Town will take over Christmas that year! Jack assigns Christmas-related jobs to the Halloween Town residents: they must sing carols, craft presents, and build a sleigh that Halloween Town reindeer — skeletal reindeer — will pull.

A prominent Halloween Town resident, the rag doll Sally, has a vision in which the efforts of Halloween Town to "do Christmas" end in disaster. Sally warns Jack about her vision but he dismisses her warning because he is so excited about the possibility of putting on Christmas. He assigns Sally to sew him a red "Sandy Claws"-style coat. The "Pumpkin King" is ruthless in getting Christmas for himself and his cohorts so he assigns a trio of trick-or-treaters called Lock, Shock, and Barrell to kidnap Santa Claus and bring him to Halloween Town. They abduct Santa who is brought to Jack who informs the kidnapped Santa that Jack Skellington will be bring the holiday of Christmas to the world this year.

Jack tells Lock, Shock, and Barrel to keep Santa prisoner but keep him safe. However, when Jack is not in sight, the trio turn poor Santa over to a gambling-loving boogeyman called Oogie Boogie who wants to play a game with Santa's life as the stakes!

Sally does not want Jack taking over Christmas (after all, she had a vision indicating this was not a good thing). She wants Santa to stop Jack. Sally tries to free Santa but, instead, finds herself another Oogie Boogie captive.

In the meantime, Jack Skellington is delivering Christmas presents to the world — but the strange, Halloween-style presents shock and frighten the recipients. Radio reports are broadcast that Santa Claus has been replaced by an imposter. Military forces shoot down Jack who crash lands — appropriately enough — in a cemetery!

Jack realizes that Christmas is not the holiday that he can create. However, remembering the shrieks of terror with which people reacted to his gifts leads him to a fresh appreciation of Halloween. He decides he must set things right, giving Christmas back to Santa Claus and Christmas Town. When he gets back to Halloween Town, Oogie Boogie tries to destroy ('kill" might not be the right word since Jack is a skeleton!) Jack. Our resourceful Jack pulls apart the thread that holds the cloth form of Oogie Boogie together — and Oogie is shown to be a massive collection of bugs! The insects fall into Oogie Boogie's own cauldron. To Santa, Jack says he is very sorry for having Santa kidnapped and for having made such a mess of Christmas. Santa is still sore — Jack had him abducted, after all — but he tells Jack things will be all right.

And they are. Santa Claus goes back to Christmas Town. Santa replaces Jack's Halloween-style presents with traditionally Christmas-style presents. Halloween Town celebrates because Jack Skellington, their Pumpkin King leader, is back. Then Santa Claus pays a voluntary visit to Halloween Town in which he brings a snowfall. The residents happily play in that snow. The film ends on a romantic note as Jack and Sally acknowledge that they are in love.

Danny Elfman has a surname peculiarly appropriate to someone who contributed to a Christmas film — although he never voiced an elf in this flick! A Jew, Elfman contributed to *The Nightmare Before Christmas* in several ways. While Chris Sarandon provided Jack Skellington's speaking voice, Elfman was his singing voice. He was the voice of Barrel and that of The Clown with the Tear-Away Face. He also wrote the score for the film and ten of its songs!

Elfman was born in 1953 in Los Angeles, California. His ancestors were Jews who immigrated to America from Poland and Russia. He was raised in an affluent neighborhood. He loved motion pictures from a young age and regularly frequented local movie theaters. In the early 1970s, Elfman served as musical director for a street theater performance art troupe called The Mystic Knights of the Oingo Boingo, a group in which his brother Richard worked. In 1979, Richard decided to leave the troupe for filmmaking. But before doing so, he made a film of the group giving performances. That film was titled *Forbidden Zone*. Danny Elfman composed songs and the score for the film and appeared at a piano as "Satan" playing a slightly altered version of Cab Calloway's song, "Minnie the Moocher."

After Richard exited the group, Danny took over as lead singer and songwriter and shortened the unwieldy name to just Oingo Boingo. The group toured and recorded as a New Wave band. Danny Elfman disbanded the group in 1995, partly because he had suffered damage to his hearing from the group's performances.

Elfman made an enormous splash in motion pictures when he wrote the score for *Pee-wee's Big Adventure* (1985). Success followed success as he scored films and won the 1989 Grammy for Tim Burton's *Batman*. Elfman has often scored Burton films, has worked with many other top directors, and has received Academy Award nominations for several movie scores. He has written music for concerts and stage productions. He has also contributed mightily to television, authoring themes for *The Simpsons*, *Tales from the Crypt*, *The Flash*, and *Desperate Housewives*. His theme for *Desperate Housewives* garnered Elfman his first Emmy.

Another Jewish individual who contributed to *The Nightmare Before Christmas* is Paul Reubens who voiced Lock. Reubens and Burton had previously worked together on *Batman Returns* (1992) and had also worked together on the film in which Reubens starred *Pee-wee's Big Adventure* (1985).

Paul Reubens was born Paul Rubenfeld in 1952 to Milton and Judy Rubenfeld. Although born in Peekskill, New York, he grew up in Sarasota, Florida. His mother was a schoolteacher. His father worked as a car salesperson when Paul was a child. Milton was also a pilot who had flown in the military in World War II. He was also one of the founding pilots of the Israeli Air Force and served during the 1948 Arab-Israeli War.

Reubens often went to circuses as a child. The circus planted the seeds for much of his adult work. He loved watching *I Love Lucy* re-runs and decided he wanted a career in comedy because he wanted to make people laugh.

As a young adult in the 1970s, he often performed at comedy clubs and made multiple guest appearances on *The Gong Show*, a TV contest-variety show. He worked with an improvisational comedy group called The Groundlings. Phil Hartman was also in the group and the two worked on material together.

In a 1978 improv exercise, Reubens invented a character with whom he would become solidly identified, the child-man Pee-wee Herman. Indeed, Reubens attained stardom on the basis of *The Pee-wee Herman Show* (1981-1984). An odd part of the odd character was that Reubens wanted people to think of Pee-wee Herman as an actual person.

The character of Pee-wee Herman not only helped make its creator famous, but led to fame for Tim Burton as well when the film starring Reubens and entitled *Pee-Wee's Big Adventure* (1985) catapulted Burton to fame. It seems only fitting that they would work together on *The Nightmare Before Christmas*.

Pee-wee's Big Adventure led to the children's TV show *Pee-wee's Playhouse* (1986-1991). In the show, Reubens tried to teach morality to children as he entertained them so episodes often emphasized matters like the need for cooperation. The show also strived for racial diversity.

In 1991, the world of Paul Reubens came crashing down in a bitterly ironic way. He was in an adult film theater and police officer arrested him for masturbating in public. That he had been a performer primarily known for children's shows, and played a character named Pee-wee, made the rather sad situation ripe for jokes. Indeed, Reubens himself poked fun at the situation when he appeared as Pee-wee at the 1991 MTV Video Music Awards and cheekily asked the audience, "Heard any good jokes lately?" The self-mocking witticism provoked a standing ovation!

Reubens pled no contest in November 1991. The charge would not enter into his record and he would do 75 hours of community service. He kept a relatively low profile during the 1990s but appeared on various programs including the highly rated TV series *Murphy Brown*. In 2001, he played a hairdresser/dope dealer in the film *Blow*.

He was hit with another round of ironic legal troubles in 2002. Police investigated him for possession of child pornography. A longtime collector of kitsch memorabilia, there were reports that he had kiddie porn as well as classic collectibles. With a search warrant, police went to his home to investigate.

Reubens was charged with possession of obscene material featuring a child under the age of 18. However, after examining the items in the collection, the district attorney decided against bringing felony charges against the performer. Nonetheless, city attorney Rocky Delgadillo brought misdemeanor charges against Reubens. Represented by attorney Blair Berk, Reubens entered a not guilty plea. In March 2004, child porn charges were dropped in exchange for Reubens' agreement to plead guilty to a lesser charge.

The scandal-arrest repeat must have been a major headache for Reubens, but it did not derail his career. Throughout the 2000s and 2010s, Reubens appeared in various entertainment projects. He is a highly sought after and very busy performer as of this writing.

Elf (2003)

This twenty-first century motion picture is a light-hearted and loving film, a fantasy-comedy-romance that begins in an orphanage (Charles Dickens, anyone?) with a baby boy entranced by the sight of a teddy bear in the sack of Santa Claus (Ed Asner). Going after the toy, the infant crawls into Santa Claus's sack without Santa's knowledge. Santa unknowingly transports the human infant back to the North Pole. When Santa's elves find a little human baby has unknowingly tagged along, they see the brand name "Buddy" on his diaper and name him Buddy. Papa Elf (Bob Newhart) adopts and raises Buddy as his son. The fantasy premise of the film — a human raised in a North Pole community of Santa's elves — give the filmmakers the opportunity for the sort of "fish out of water" scenarios that are so rich in comic gold. That gold is mined throughout the film with vigor and vim.

Although the other elves treat him as one of their own, his human size means he has trouble doing the usual elf jobs. Recognizing his inefficiency, Buddy says despairingly, "I'm a cotton-headed ninnymuggins." An elf, Ming-Ming (Peter Billingsley) tries to reassure him that he is "special" and has "special talents." All the elves are sympathetic to Buddy and try make him feel valued and accepted despite the special difficulties he has. His problems keeping up the toy making pace lead to his re-assignment as a toy tester.

One day, Buddy overhears some elves talking about him and his special problems. One comments, "If he hasn't figured out he's a human by now, I don't think he ever will." A clearly shocked Buddy flashes back to all the times he stuck out like a sore thumb among elves due to his human size. An elf asks if he is all right and Buddy assures him he is — right before falling upon the elf in a dead faint!

Papa Elf, who has been an adoptive father to Buddy, tells him the story of his origins. He was born the human child of Susan Wells and Walter Hobbs who made an adoption plan for him. Susan died shortly after placing him for adoption; Walter is alive and working for a children's book publisher in New York City. However, Walter does not even know Buddy exists.

Buddy desperately wants to meet his biological father. He asks Santa for information about New York City and Santa tells him not to pick up gum from the street "because it's not free candy" and that if he spots a sign reading "Peep Show," that is not a place that gives advance peeks into Christmas gifts. Then Santa lets Buddy know some devastating news about his Dad.

"He's on the Naughty List," Santa states. "

NOOOOOOO!" Buddy cries in horror as the camera goes to Santa's book of Lists and the name "Walter Hobbs" is highlighted. Santa explains that Walter has been acting in an unscrupulous manner. However, Santa adds that it might be possible for Buddy to redeem Walter and help him make it to the Nice List.

A hopeful Buddy, garbed in his green elf outfit with toe-turned-up shoes, arrives in New York City. Again, the "fish out of water" theme is brilliantly mined for, just as Buddy stuck out in the world of Santa and the elves because of his humanity, his socialization as an elf means that he is an adult man who appears comically childlike and awkward in the human world.

Buddy finds Walter Hobbs (James Caan) in his work office. Buddy explains that he is his long-lost son, the baby he sired with Susan Wells, but Walter assumes the oddly dressed fellow before him is there to deliver a singing Christmas-gram. Walter's fellow employees stare at Buddy with a mix of bafflement and amusement as Buddy sings off-key to his father. Believing Buddy an annoying mental case, Walter has him escorted off the premises.

Soon Buddy finds himself in a department store. Unfamiliar with escalators, he does a kind of "split" with his legs stretched out from one step of the escalator to another. The manager assumes from Buddy's colorful apparel that he is working there as a Christmas elf. The manager directs him to the store's Santa Land. Buddy sees a pretty worker, Jovie (Zooey Deschanel), and immediately has the warm fuzzies for her.

Buddy learns that Santa will be at the store tomorrow! He is jubilant as he decorates Santa Land. Looking forward to seeing his old friend, Buddy runs up to the man sitting in front of a bunch of kids sporting a thick curly white beard and garbed in red and white. Then Buddy realizes that the department store Santa is not the real one! "Who are you?" he asks.

"I'm Santa Claus," the store employee answers as a small child approaches him.

When the store Santa asks the child what he wants for Christmas, Buddy interrupts to warn the child that this is not Santa. Buddy adds to the man, "You stink! You smell like beef and cheese! You don't smell like Santa!"

Then Buddy pulls on the man's thick curly white Santa Clause beard — and it easily comes off in Buddy's hand!

"He's a faker!" Buddy exclaims as the children scream.

The understandably upset department store Santa gets into a terrific fight with Buddy as the little kids continue screaming. The wild melee leads Buddy to the inside of a jail cell.

Walter bails Buddy out of jail and the pair head to a clinic for a DNA test. The results of the test lead Walter to acknowledge Buddy as his long-lost son. Thus, Walter takes his adult son home to meet Walter's wife Emily (Mary Steenburgen) as well as Walter's other son — and Buddy's half-brother — Michael (Daniel Tay). Michael, like his Dad, is disconcerted by Buddy's "elf" ways, but Emily feels an immediate compassion for a young man she perceives as mentally ill.

Michael and Buddy are eventually able to forge a brotherly connection and Michael encourages Buddy to ask Jovie for a date. She accepts and they fall in love.

The focus switches to Walter's work troubles. The last book the company put out failed to make money. Hard-driving boss Fulton Greenway (Michael Lerner) tells Walter he must have a new book ready by Christmas Eve. Walter and other employees meet with Miles Finch (Peter Dinklage), a successful author of children's books — and a dwarf. Buddy intrudes into the meeting to blissfully announce that he is in love.

Seeing Finch's dwarf stature, a smiling Buddy exclaims, "I didn't know you had elves working here!"

Understandably offended but believing that Buddy is trying to be funny, a frowning Finch points out that no one is laughing.

Of course, Buddy had no intention of being funny when he made the initial comment. Nor does he have any intention of being funny when he inquires, "Does Santa know that you left the workshop? Did you need a reindeer to get here?"

Boiling mad, Finch throws his financial success in Buddy's face and dares him to call him an elf again. Having no idea that he is even insulting Finch, Buddy comments, "He's an angry elf."

The outraged dwarf jumps onto the desk and marches over to Buddy who seems clueless about the man's obviously violent intentions. Finch attacks the shocked Buddy who, despite his vast superiority in size, is no match for Finch's fury. After giving Buddy a thorough drubbing, Finch storms out of the room even as Walter begs the writer to stay.

Walter turns on Buddy in rage. He tells him he does not care if the man is his son or if he is mentally ill but only wants him out of his life for good. Outraged at Buddy's behavior, Walter disowns him.

Crestfallen, Buddy leaves a note to Walter, Emily, and Michael on an etch-a-sketch in which Buddy expresses a terrible sense of alienation because of his inability to fit into any environment.

Walter finds a notebook Finch kept of ideas so Walter and his co-workers brainstorm a book idea to pitch. When Walter returns home, Michael tells him of Buddy's note and Buddy's absence. Overcome with remorse for disowning his son, Walter tells off Greenway who promptly fires him. Then Walter and Michael search for Buddy.

Desolate and despairing, Buddy wanders the streets until he sees Santa Claus's sleigh crash in Central Park! As might be expected, a large and curious crowd gathers round. Buddy finds Santa Claus who reveals that the sleigh lost its engine and is unable to fly sans engine because of a shortage of Christmas spirit! Buddy finds the engine (shades of a reindeer called Rudolph?).

Walter and Michael find Buddy. The three lovingly reunite. Buddy introduces his father and half-brother to Santa Claus. Michael knows this is the real Santa because the white-bearded and red-coated fellow shows Michael what he wanted for Christmas. Michael proves to the world that Santa is real by reading the List as news cameras film the reading. The Central Park Rangers are upset to find themselves on the Naughty Side of the List so they chase the sleigh as Buddy tries to put the engine back inside.

Jovie leads the crowd in singing *Santa Claus Is Coming To Town*, helping raise enough Christmas spirit to power the engine-less sleigh.

The film hurtles forward to the next Christmas: Walter has his own publishing company, known for a best-seller about Buddy's life; Buddy and Jovie are married and bring their first baby to visit Papa Elf.

The considerable Christmas Spirit of *Elf* was powered by several folks from the Chanukah crew. Director Jonathan Favreau was the product of a Gentile-Jewish marriage: father was of Italian and French-Canadian ancestry while mother was Jewish. Born in 1966, he was raised in his mother's faith, attending Hebrew School as a child and being Bar Mitzvahed.

Favreau's high intelligence was recognized early and he attended the Bronx High School of Science, an institution for "gifted" pupils. After graduating high school, he attended Queens College before dropping out in 1987. While in college, he was nicknamed "Johnny Hack" because he was good at the game Hacky Sack. He worked, went back to college, and dropped out for good a few credits shy of his degree in 1988 when he moved to Chicago where he started a career as a comedian, performing at improvisational theaters. He has since built a very successful career as an actor, producer, screenwriter, and (of course) director. *Elf* was his first smash financial success. His Jewish roots are evident in the name of the TV production business he founded in August, 2018: Golem Creations. In Jewish folklore, a golem is an animated human-like creature created from inanimate matter such as mud or clay.

The screenwriter for *Elf* is David Berenbaum. Born in Philadelphia, Berenbaum had a small part in *Elf* as a Greenway officer worker. His writing credits include a Disney film entitled *The Haunted Mansion* (2003) that starred Eddie Murphy and *Strange Magic* (2015). Berenbaum seems to have an especially warm spot in his heart for Christmas as it has been reported that he sold a script entitled *Christmas in New Jersey* that is in development as of this book's writing.

A true star, James Caan was born in the Bronx to Jewish parents, Arthur Caan and Sophie Caan, née Falkenstein, both of whom immigrated from Germany. Strong and athletic from his early years, James Caan was a rodeo rider in his youth who was nicknamed "The Jewish Cowboy." When the acting bug bit, Caan appeared in theatrical productions prior to his motion picture debut in 1963 in *Irma La Douce*. In 1964, Caan had his first large movie role as a young hoodlum named Randall in the shocker *Lady In A Cage*. In that tense and violent motion picture, Olivia de Havilland stars as a rich widow who becomes trapped in her own private elevator – an elevator with "bars" like a cage -- during a power outage. When she tries to get help through the elevator's emergency alarm system, she attracts instead a motley collection of home invaders including Caan's nasty Randall. Caan went on to Hollywood stardom through the Western *El Dorado* (1967) where he worked alongside Hollywood greats John Wayne and Robert Mitchum. He delivered a brilliant performance as Chicago Bears football player Brian Piccolo in the made-for-TV movie *Brian's Song* (1971); the film was a well-made tearjerker that dealt with Piccolo's early death from cancer. Caan went on to garner accolades for his performance as gangster Sonny Corleone in *The Godfather* (1972) and *The Godfather: Part II* (1974). Since then, he has made a variety of successful motion pictures including *Alien Nation* (1988), *Dick Tracy* (1990), *Misery* (1990), *Eraser* (1999), *The Yards* (2000), *Dogville* (2003).

Ed Asner is a star probably best-known to the public for his depiction of newspaper editor Lou Grant first in the TV comedy *The Mary Tyler Moore Show* and then in its spin-off drama *Lou Grant*. Asner was born in 1929 in Kansas City, Missouri and spent most of his formative years in Kansas City, Kansas (he sure kept it Kansas!). Raised in an Orthodox Jewish family, he served in the U.S. Army in his youth. Already interested in acting, he appeared in plays that toured Army camps. After he wound up military service, he headed for New York City where he was busy acting in theater plays. His TV debut was in 1957 on *Studio One* and followed with roles in a 1963 episode of *The Outer Limits* and a 1965 episode of *Voyage to the Bottom of the Sea*.

He played a variety of roles on TV throughout the 1960s before landing the plum role of Lou Grant on *The Mary Tyler Moore Show*, a groundbreaking slice of life comedy. What made it special was that the main character was a single career-oriented woman, something rare in TV sitcoms before that point. Indeed, his chief fame rested on his depiction of Grant in that comedy.

Oddly, the spin-off, *Lou Grant*, in which he was the star, was *not* a comedy but a straight drama. There was at least one episode of *Lou Grant* that might have hit home in a special way for Asner. That episode was entitled "Nazi." It was based on the real-life tragedy of Dan Burros, an emotionally disturbed Jewish man who, at one point in his life, actually joined the American Nazi Party. (Is it even necessary to point out that a Jew who would join such a group would be emotionally disturbed?) During his time with the Nazis, he was seen as "weird" even by his cohorts because he liked to regale them with fantasies he had of having a Jewish person linked up to the strings of a piano which was in turn linked up to a torture device. In this fantasy, Burros imagined the victim being tortured in tune to the playing of the piano. He also had a habit of walking around with an ordinary bar of soap on which he had affixed the label "Made from the Finest Jewish Fat." His fellow Nazis began to suspect his Jewish background and he parted company with them. However, he had not left anti-Semitism behind as he then joined up with a Ku Klux Klan group called the United Klans of America (UKA)! He was a Kleagon, or recruiter, for the KKK group when a *New York Times* reporter uncovered evidence of his Jewish ethnicity. The reporter called Burros and offered to not run the story *if* Burros agreed to abandon racism and anti-Semitism. Burros refused that offer. *The New York Times* ran the story that the Kleagon of a KKK group was Jewish. Burros committed suicide.

The story in *Lou Grant* was changed slightly. The Burros stand-in was a Nazi with a swastika on his arm — as Burros had been but was not when the *NYT* "outed" him — rather than a Klansman sporting a white hood.

Reporter Billie Newman (Linda Kelsey) investigates a group of American Nazis led by Commander Donald Stryker (Peter Weller). She decides to probe Stryker's background and learns that he changed his name from Donald Sterner, that his parents are Jewish, and he was bar mitzvahed. When Billie's article about Stryker's Jewish ethnicity is published, he commits suicide like his real-life model. Billie is shattered but Grant reassures her that she did a good job and newspapers cannot refrain from publishing stories because "someone might get hurt" as that is an inevitable part of the business.

Asner played Captain Davies in the acclaimed mini-series *Roots* and won an Emmy for that performance. He also won an Emmy for playing in *Rich Man, Poor Man* (1976). The Jewish actor played a Pope in an Italian made-for-TV movie entitled *Pope John XXIII* (2002). An accomplished voice actor, he vocalized a major character in the Academy Award-winning *Up* (2009).

Asner is a strong and longtime supporter of The Survivor Mitzvah Project, a charity that provides aid to elderly and impoverished Holocaust survivors. According to the Project's website, "In 2012, [Asner] lent his considerable talents to two Survivor Mitzvah Project Programs at The Simon Wiesenthal Center's Museum of Tolerance: *IN THEIR OWN WORDS* for *International Holocaust Remembrance Day* and The Survivor Mitzvah Project Fundraiser, *THE STARS COME OUT FOR SURVIVORS* where he read Holocaust testimonies from survivors from Lithuania, Belarus, and Ukraine."

The Night Before (2015): Potheads Celebrate Christmas

Who would have guessed that a Christmas movie would also be a "stoner film"? A Christmas motion picture tied to the illegal drug culture appears a perverse idea on the surface. Perhaps it is that very perversity that led to *The Night Before* (2015). After all, creativity often means juxtaposing things that are so unalike that their union catches imaginative fire.

The stoner film came into its own in the late 1970s-mid 1980s with the Cheech & Chong series of movies in which comedy team Richard "Cheech" Marin and Tommy Chong released a series of motion pictures, beginning with *Up In Smoke* (1978) about the adventures of pot smokers. Since that auspicious beginning, "stoner films" have become a film sub-genre with a kind of guaranteed following in the multitude of people who seek to change consciousness and/or mood through chemical means other than the more "Establishment" ways such as alcohol. Indeed, *High Times* magazine regularly sponsors the Stoner Awards to celebrate films that prominently feature drug-taking characters and situations revolving around drugs.

The Night Before was directed by Jonathan Levine who co-wrote its screenplay along with writers Evan Goldberg, Kyle Hunter, and Ariel Shaffir. The story of the film begins in December 2001 when the parents of Ethan Miller (Joseph Gordon-Levitt) are killed in a tragic car accident. His best buddies, Isaac Greenberg (Seth Rogen) and Chris Roberts (Anthony Mackie) make a promise that they will spend every Christmas Eve ever after with Ethan.

However, in 2015, Isaac and Chris decide they should end this practice. Both men just have too many other demands on their time and energy to be devoting the Christmas season to Ethan: Isaac is married and his wife is pregnant: Chris is a famous football player. They worry that Ethan has become so dependent on this yearly practice that he cannot stand for it to end. But his pals want 2015 to be the last Christmas Eve the trio spend together.

By the time the majority of events take place, Ethan is yearning for music stardom but supporting himself by working at a hotel. At his job, he steals invitations to the Nutcracker Ball.

The three gather at Isaac's home. Isaac's wife Betsy (Jillian Bell) knows her husband and his friends are inveterate users of mood-altering pharmaceuticals so she gives Isaac drugs, including cocaine, for him to take (and possibly share) at his leisure. After Isaac receives this gift, the buddies follow previous custom with an initial stop at the Rockefeller Tree. Ethan shows Chris and Isaac the Nutcracker Ball invitations!

Chris buys marijuana (this is a stoner movie after all) from Mr. Green (Michael Shannon), a schoolteacher who had taught the friends in high school. The pals visit a karaoke bar. Other events follow but one of the most crushing (again: stoner movie) is that a Christmas-hater (Ilana Glazer) steals the pot from Chris!

Bereft of the beloved weed, the group contacts Mr. Green and replenishes their marijuana supply. Other tribulations follow until — egads! — the weed is stolen a second time!

A Jewish-Christian collision takes place when Isaac attends Midnight Mass. Sick from the drug mixture he took, he vomits during the service! He also realizes that he has entered a church wearing a shirt with a big Star of David on its front. It is hard to say what embarrasses him more.

The Night Before pulls out all the wackiness stops with a stoner film meets *It's a Wonderful Life* twist – followed by a second twist.

This flamboyant stoner film-Christmas film honors Christmas even as it melds the love and generosity of this holiday with the "druggie" subculture. Just as noteworthy is the way it takes witty aim at inevitable culture clashes between Christians and Jews. It would be tempting to interpret this as a consequence of the Christmas-loving film's having such a high Semitic representation among those who contributed to it. Those of Hebrew ethnicity/faith include the director (Jonathan Levine), at least two of its three producers (Evan Goldberg, Seth Rogan), at least three of its four screenwriters (Jonathan Levine, Ariel Shaffir, Evan Goldberg), and at least six of its major performers (Joseph Gordon-Levitt, Seth Rogen, Lizzy Caplan, Ilana Glazer, Nathan Fielder).

In 1976 Jonathan Levine was born into a Jewish family living in New York City. Success came early and easily to him. He earned a Masters of Fine Arts (MF) in Film Directing from the American Film Institute in Los Angeles, California. His AFI Thesis short film, *Shards* (2004), won a Certificate of Excellence for Best Cinematography at the 2005 Brooklyn Film Festival (Petra Korner was the cinematographer on the short).

All the Boys Love Mandy Lane (2006), a horror movie, was the first feature film Levine directed. His best-known film may be *50/50*, starring Seth Rogen, Amy Kendrick, and Joseph Gordon-Levitt, about a man who seems to be a model of health and fitness but finds his world turned upside down by a cancerous tumor. The film garnered several awards including the Audience Award at the 2011 Aspen Filmfest. Other directing efforts include *Warm Bodies* (2013), a film about a zombie who returns to being a normal human. Levine maintains a busy schedule as a director, screenwriter, and producer.

Evan Goldberg is a Canadian and was born in 1982 in Vancouver, British Columbia. As a child, he and Seth Rogen were friends and that friendship has apparently continued through their lives. The two of them have collaborated as writers on several films and have formed their own production company called Point Grey Pictures. Both Goldberg and Rogen have described themselves as "obsessed" fans of the TV cartoon comedy *The Simpsons*. They collaborated on the writing of a *Simpsons* episode entitled "Homer the Whopper." Goldberg's recent endeavors include acting as executive producer on TV series *Future Man (*2017-2019) and *The Boys* (2019).

Seth Rogen, like his good friend Evan Goldberg, was born in Canada. Also like Goldberg, Rogen was born in 1982. His parents, Sandy Rogen (née Belongs) and Mark Rogen, met in a kibbutz in Israel. They raised their son in Vancouver, British Columbia. Sandy Rosen was a social worker and Mark Rogen was Assistant Director of the Jewish fraternal organization, the Workman's Circle.

Deciding on a career in comedy while but a child, the red-haired Seth Rogen brought his heritage into his early comedy routines, often using his bar mitzvah as a launching pad for jokes. Indeed, bar mitzvahs, along with other small gatherings. were a frequent setting for the comedy routines of the teenaged Rogen. He and Evan Goldberg met at their bar mitzvah classes.

Rogen made his professional acting debut in the NBC TV series *Freaks and Geeks* that was about teenagers. It was canceled after one season due to low ratings but has become a cult series. He played in films *Donnie Darko* (2001) and *Anchorman: The Legend of Ron Burgundy* (2004) and was a staff writer for Sacha Baron Cohen for the 2004 last season of *Da Ali G Show*. Rogen acted in and co-produced *The 40-Year-Old Virgin* (2005).

Knocked Up (2007), a comedy, the plot of which is made clear in the title, gave Rogen his first role as a leading man. The film was a big hit with both critics and public so it gave Rogen's career a real boost. He has done voice work in such films as *Horton Hears a Who!* (2008) and *The Spiderwick Chronicles*. He also did voice work in the science fiction comedy *Paul* (2011). He has hosted *Saturday Night Live* multiple times and has a very busy schedule.

Ariel Shaffir is not only a screenwriter but also an actor, comedian, producer, and podcaster. Shaffir's father and grandmother were Holocaust survivors. He was born in New York City but spent much of his childhood in North Carolina. When he was nine years old, the family made two major changes: relocating to Maryland and switching from Conservative Judaism to Orthodox Judaism.

After graduating from the University of Maryland, Shaffir move to Los Angeles, California because he believed it was a better place to be a stand-up comedian. In the late 2000s, Shaffir spent much of his time on comedy tours. In 2012, he released a comedy album entitled *Revenge for the Holocaust*. As an actor, he often appeared in TV commercials, plugging such businesses as Subway and Dominos and such products as Bud Light. In 2017, he said he lost interest in acting and prefers stand-up comedy.

Joseph Gordon-Levitt was born in Los Angeles, California in 1981. He has described his Jewish parents as "not strictly religious." His mother and father helped found a group called the Progressive Jewish Alliance. His mother, Jane Gordon, ran for Congress during the 1970s on the Peace and Freedom Party ticket. His father, Dennis Levitt, spent part of his working life as news director for a radio station.

Gordon-Levitt was only four years old when he played the Scarecrow in a staging of *The Wizard of Oz*. Just a preschooler, he was off to a wonderful start and made appearances in TV shows and commercials. In 1991, he acted in the revived *Dark Shadows* TV Gothic soap opera. He made a huge splash as Tommy Solomon on the TV show *3rd Rock from the Sun*; a witty critic observed that he was "a Jewish kid pretending to be an extraterrestrial pretending to be a Jewish kid."

He stopped acting with the turn of the century to attend Columbia University. In 2004, he dropped out and went back to acting. He played in a wide variety of films and branched out into directing and producing.

Lizzy Caplan was born in 1982 in L.A. Her family practiced Reform Judaism. She began her acting career in 1999 with a part in the TV series *Freaks and Geeks*. She was in the music video *You and I Both* and played in such TV series as *Once and Again* and *The Pitts* and was in films such as *Mean Girls* (2004). She played Virginia Johnson in the Showtime series *Masters of Sex*.

Born in 1987, Ilana Glazer is probably best known for both co-creating and co-starring in the Comedy Central series *Broad City*. She grew up in St. James, New York. Her family were Reform Jews. Along with *The Night Before*, she has acted in the indie film *How To Follow Strangers* and the comedy *Rough Night* (2017).

Nathan Fiedler is a Canadian and was born in 1983. His parents, Eric and Deb Fiedler, were social workers. During his teen years, he began performing as a magician. He started his comedy career in the mid-2000s. In 2013, he created his own Comedy Central show called *Nathan For You*.

After learning that the Canadian company Taiga posted a tribute to a Holocaust denier, Fielder began a non-profit company he named Summit Ice Apparel in 2015. The company produces soft shell jackets. Its profits go to the Vancouver Holocaust Education Centre. That is a certainly a commendable cause since there are, in fact, still people denying the reality of this proven historical tragedy.

The Flight Before Christmas (2015)

A made-for-TV movie, *The Flight Before Christmas* tells the story of Stephanie (Mayim Bialik) who is about to start living with her boyfriend (Gib Gerard) when — wouldn't you know it? — he breaks up with her. It is also right before Christmas so she is nursing a broken heart at what should be a time of joy. She decides to fly home to Connecticut to spend the holidays with her family.

On the plane, she finds herself seated beside Michael (Ryan McPartlin). They start chatting and she learns he wants to propose marriage to his girlfriend. The seat mates get into a little quarrel. Then the pilot announces that a snowstorm necessitates the plane stop in Bozeman, Montana. Enjoying a bit of good luck (for a change), Stephanie manages to get the last available room at a bed and breakfast. Despite their spat, she likes Michael so she offers to share the room with him. The two of them realize that a romantic fire is building between them. However, the recently jilted Stephanie does not want to jettison Michael's matrimonial plans. She takes off from the bed and breakfast to go to the airport. The smitten Michael searches for her and finds her at the airport. Although they say their goodbyes, Michael realizes this is true love. He breaks it off with his girlfriend and begins another search for Stephanie. The film ends with the couple kissing after a New Year's countdown.

This wonderfully cute Christmas romantic comedy has at least two major Jewish links: screenwriter Jennifer Notas Shapiro and star Mayim Bialik,

Interestingly, Jennifer Notas Shapiro penned a piece for *Grok Nation* entitled "I'm the Jew who writes Christmas movies." In that essay, she states, "While I may not celebrate Christmas, my work immerses me in the holiday spirit for much of the summer and fall." The essay's publication date, 11/27/2015, is important to keep in mind when we read Shapiro reveal, "I've made my living in the past few years writing TV movies for the Hallmark and Lifetime channels — mostly romantic comedies, and once, a 'woman in jeopardy' baby-stealing number — but this year every project I worked on was a Christmas movie."

Shapiro recalls that she penned her first Christmas TV flick in 2009. The executives informed her that the script needed "more Christmas."

"Well, tell me what else you people do," she answered. "This isn't my holiday."

The remark occasioned laughter because it is "an easy punchline, the Jew writing Christmas movies." One reason it occasions guffaws is that writers are traditionally advised to "write what you know." However, there are obvious problems with this since writers often craft stories about Martians, ghosts, vampires, and other things that most of us believe do not even exist so they can hardly be expected to "know" their material in the usual way. Shapiro concludes that the real advice writers need is to "write with care and passion and do your homework if need be." She is also certain that being Jewish is no barrier to getting the Christmas spirit down on paper: "I don't have to decorate a pine tree with tinsel in order to understand the feelings of family, togetherness, and joy that everyone wants to feel around the Christmas holiday."

The star of this show, Mayim Bialik, is also Jewish. Her birthplace was San Diego, California and the year of her birth was 1975. Raised in Reform Judaism, she was bat mitzvahed. As an adult, she has adopted what is called Modern Orthodox Judaism. Throughout her life, Judaism has been central to her identity. In 2000, she graduated from the University of California, Los Angeles with a B.S. in neuroscience; she had minors in Hebrew and in Jewish Studies.

Her acting career started in the 1980s when she was still a child. She had recurring roles in TV shows such as *The Facts of Life*, *Beauty and the Beast*, and *Webster*. In the motion picture *Beaches* (1988), she played Bette Midler's character as a kid. She played in other shows, sometimes doing voiceover work, before her casting in 2010 as Dr. Amy Farrah Fowler in the TV series *The Big Bang Theory*.

Bialik is married to Michael Stone, a man born and raised in a Mormon family who converted to Judaism. She calls herself a "staunch Zionist." In YouTube videos, she discusses Judaism. With her two sons, she lit the menorah for a 2011 Chanukah music video of an American Orthodox Jewish a cappella singing group called The Maccabeats. Of course, like many of her co-religionists, she made a beautiful entertainment contribution to Christmas even as she celebrated Chanukah on her own time.

Chapter 5
The Holiday Called Chanukah/Hanukkah

The major Jewish holiday that tends to occur in December — although it may start in November in some years — is variously spelled Chanukah or Hanukkah in English. In *The Jewish Way: Living the Holidays*, Rabbi Irving Greenberg asserts, "The story of Hanukkah really begins in the fourth century B.C.E., with Alexander the Great's invasion of the Middle East and Asia. This conquest paved the way for the blend of Greek culture and Eastern traditions that become known as Hellenism." Greenberg also states, "The empire that Alexander made possible was split into three fragments: the Macedonian kingdom in Europe; Asia (including Syria, Mesopotamia, and Persia) ruled by the Seleucids; and Egypt ruled by the Ptolemies." During the third century A.D./C.E., the Seleucid King of Syria Antiochus III captured what was then called "Palestine" and had been ruled by the Ptolemies just before he conquered it.

King Antiochus III had pro-Hebrew feelings. Greenberg writes, "Antiochus issued a charter giving a series of privileges and projects of assistance to the Jews, including help in rebuilding Jerusalem, money for supplying the Temple with sacrifices, wine, and other items, and a grant of permission to live according to their laws." Even as the Jews were officially allowed to follow their specifically Hebrew ways, some of them considered those ways backward and stultifying in comparison with the Greek culture that dominated the area. Called "Hellenists," these Jews sought to assimilate into the dominant culture, discarding Hebrew beliefs and ways for Greek. Indeed, Greenberg believes, "Had the process of Hellenization continued gradually and peacefully, it might well have taken over the Jewish people."

But the gradual and peaceful Hellenization — which could have actually divested Jews of their distinctive identity, at least in the opinion of Rabbi Greenberg — was superseded by a much different sort of Hellenization when King Antiochus IV came to the throne. He issued an edict that the Jews must stop reading and following the Torah. He decreed that Jews must stop observing the Sabbath. He decreed that they could not circumcise their male infants. To read Torah, observe the Sabbath, and circumcise boy babies were all made crimes punishable by the death penalty! The Jewish Temple in Jerusalem was required to set up a statue of Zeus, the greatest of the Greek gods. The king required that animal sacrifices to Zeus be made in that Temple. Perhaps worst of all, an animal considered traditionally "unclean" in Judaism, the pig, had to be among the sacrifices.

"Hellenizing" Jews actually welcomed these changes. But others, holding their Jewish identity precious, did not. In the small town of Modiin, a Jewish priest named Mattathias strongly — and defiantly — clung to Judaism. In the place he worshipped, a Hellenistic Jew sacrificed a pig to Zeus. Enraged, Mattathias stabbed the Hellenized Jew to death. The outraged Mattathias also killed an agent of the king and pulled down the altar defiled by pig blood. Needless to say, things soon got hot for Mattathias! Luckily for him, he had five sons to aid him. Those five youths were Yochanan, Simon, Judah, Eliezer, and Jonathan. Their Biblical names were significant since Hellenizing types of Jews tended to give their sons Greek names.

Mattathias and his sons fled to the mountains to escape the wrath of King Antiochus IV. They were joined by other Jews wanting to maintain Judaism. These fighters for Judaism became known as the Maccabees — an appropriate name as Maccabee means "hammer" in Hebrew and these valiant warriors hammered hard at their enemies. They were badly outnumbered and out-equipped by the forces of the king so the Maccabees largely engaged in guerrilla actions. Greenberg observes that they benefited from "mobility and superior knowledge of the terrain" and that their mountain base "granted them inaccessibility and allowed strategic maneuvering." Soon after the rebellion began, Mattathias died. One of his sons, Judah Maccabee, assumed leadership of the revolt.

Despite the limitations faced by the Maccabees, these dedicated soldiers fought bravely and well. They may have benefited because the army of the king had unrelated battles going on elsewhere that sapped the numbers that could be arrayed against the Maccabees. By 165 A.D./C.E., Judah had cut Jerusalem off from the Seleucid forces. The king felt it necessary to settle with the Jews. He granted the Maccabee fighters amnesty from prosecution for their revolt and gave the Jews the right to observe their faith and customs. Despite these victories, the forces of the king were still in control of much of Jerusalem — and of its all-important Temple.

Another war broke out and the Seleucid military went off to fight it. Judah saw his chance and took it: he and his men captured the city and its Temple, driving the Greco-Syrian forces and Hellenizers out of it. The Maccabees had to be appalled by what their enemies had done to their beautiful Temple. As Karla Kuskin reports in *A Great Miracle Happened There*, "They destroyed the holy scrolls and books and took the Temple's treasures. They scraped the gold from the Temple walls. Then they made a Greek temple of the place." Once the Jews had their beloved Temple back, they immediately worked to clean the place and make it beautiful and holy once again.

In what is now called the Rededication of the Temple, the Hebrew priests blessed the Temple and all that was in it. One thing they were happy to find still in this sacred building was its menorah. In Exodus 25:31-40, it is stated that God commanded Moses to build a lamp stand of pure gold with several specifications including branches extending from it that has a cup from which a candle can be lighted in the middle with three branches with similar cups extending on each side so that there are seven candle holders altogether on this sacred lamp stand. The Jews sought oil with which to light the menorah. "The celebration required the purest oil for the menorah," Seymour Chwast writes in *The Miracle of Hanukkah*. "The Maccabees found only one sealed flask of oil, enough to last just one day. But the oil burned for eight days!" This miracle was taken as a sign that the God of Judaism was still with the Jews.

Thus, the holiday called Chanukah was born. It has been observed in Jewish households for well over two thousand years and is observed to this day.

"The festival [of Chanukah] begins on the 25th day of the Hebrew month of Kislev which occurs in either late November or in December," Rabbi Dr. Shmuel Himelstein explains in *The Jewish Primer: Questions and Answers on Jewish Faith and Culture*. "It is on this day that the Temple was rededicated." Indeed, "Chanukah" is Hebrew for "dedication."

During the eight days of Chanukah, celebrants recite prayers and read from the Torah. The lighting of the menorah is probably the most significant Chanukah activity. The Chanukah menorah differs from the previously described menorah as the Talmud forbids the use of a seven-cup menorah outside a temple. Rather, the Chanukah menorah has nine candle receptacles with one being higher in position than the others and called the "shamash." On the first night of Chanukah, the most extreme right candle is lit. On the next, two candles are lit. Then it progresses each night until the wicks of all eight candles boast little flames. Blessings are recited before the lightings. "Shamash" means "assistant" or "sexton." That candle is lit and then used to light the other candles.

Although Judaism forbids gambling, a kind of "gambling" is permitted during Chanukah. Families typically gather around the table to spin the four-sided Chanukah "dreidel." The stakes are matchsticks or pennies and each person puts the same number of matchsticks or pennies into the pot. The results of the dreidel roll decide if a person will get the winnings, get half the winnings, get nothing, or have to add to the pot. Dreidels are of two forms with one used in Israel and the other used everywhere else. Each side has a word in Hebrew. In most of the world, those words translate to "A Great Miracle Happened There." In Israel, they translate to "A Great Miracle Happened Here."

Since the holiday celebrates a miracle associated with oil, it is appropriate that foods served for Chanukah are those fried in oil. Ashkenazi Jews are apt to serve "latkes," which are oil-fried potatoes, and Sephardic Jews tend to favor oil-friend donuts filled with jam. Rabbi Dr. Himelstein wryly remarks, "Hanukkah is not for dieters!"

It has long been customary for parents to give small amounts of money, known as Chanukah money, during Chanukah. These has evolved into a practice of giving children gifts for each day of Chanukah, making it a kind of eight-day Christmas! The association of gift giving with Chanukah is acknowledged by many people to be the result of the fact that Chanukah falls so close to Christmas. Rabbi Dr. Himelstein observes that, in the Western world, "where the members of the different religions all mingle freely," the result has been "a tremendous degree of adaptation and 'borrowing' between the different religious groups, and the idea of the exchange of gifts on Hanukkah is no doubt part of that adaptation." Rabbi Greenberg comments, "American Jews have turned Hanukkah into the great gift holiday." Gifts were not a major part of this holiday for centuries, but, Rabbi Greenberg continues, "Christmas is so pervasive in America and the children's sense of being shut out was so fierce that Hanukkah was rededicated as the season for giving." This must delight the Jewish children who relish their Chanukah presents as much as their neighbors love their Christmas presents!

Chanukah songs do not glut the radio waves in December as Christmas songs most certainly do, but there are many songs about Chanukah. On the *My Jewish Learning* website, MJL observes, "Hanukkah songs are a joyous and integral part of the experience of celebrating the Festival of Lights. Whether it's singing around the menorah or just rocking out together, songs play a vital role in brightening the happiness of the holiday." Amy Deutsch writes, "Maybe it's the Christmas 'competition,' but it seems like there are more songs about Hanukkah than about any other Jewish holiday." Deutsch continues that the proximity of Christmas may not be the only reason for Chanukah songs as the special characteristics of the holiday are apt to inspire songwriters: "It's fun and delicious and lasts for eight amazing days." Sophie Smith acknowledges "Christmas songs will rule the airwaves" but adds that "there are some pretty great songs that pay tribute to the Festival of Lights."

Classic Chanukah songs include "Maoz Tzur (Rock of Ages)" from thirteenth century A.D./C.E. There is also a tune with lyrics inspired by the traditional Chanukah liturgy entitled "Al Hanisim." The Chanukah song "Mi Yimalel" is inspired by Psalm 106:2 while "Hanerot Hallalu (We Must Light The Lights)" draws from Soferim 20:6 of the Talmud. Singing in Yiddish, the great performer Theodore Bikel did a memorable rendition of "Chanukah, Oy Chanukah" and the Klezmer Conservatory Band has also recorded an excellent version of the song. The song is also sung in English as "Oh Hanukkah."

The incomparable folk rock trio, Peter, Paul, and Mary, released a lovely Chanukah tribute entitled "Light One Candle." "I Have A Little Dreidel" is a children's song written in 1927 by Samuel S. Grossman and Samuel E. Goldfarb. The song begins, "I have a little dreidel/I made it out of clay/And when it's dry and ready/Then dreidel I shall play." The endearing song of the double Samuel duo has been recorded by several musical artists including *The Maccabeats* and *Barenaked Ladies*. Matisyahu, an American Jewish musician who records in a dazzling diversity of forms including reggae and rap, sings the reggae-style "Miracle" to honor Chanukah. Kenny Ellis brought out an album entitled *Hanukkah Swings* full of songs about the holiday spiced with a Big Band flavor. As well as "I Have A Little Dreidel," *The Maccabeats* have recorded Chanukah songs like "Candlelight" and "We're All About that Neis, No Oil." In the last song, "neis" means "test" or "banner," both of which are appropriate for the Chanukah miracle.

Sprightly pop-style songs with a comic bent can liven up the characteristically quite lively holiday called Chanukah. Rachel Bloom, Jack Dolmen, and Dan Gregor released *Suck It, Christmas!* an album full of humorous Chanukah songs. Adam Sandler's "The Hanukkah Song" says it was explicitly written for the youngster who feels like "you're the only kid without a Christmas tree" and it lightheartedly lists some of the better-known Jewish celebrities. Mr. Palindrome sings a lively parody of a comical Christmas song, "I Want A Hippopotamus For Hanukkah." The band called the LeeVees brought out the whimsical "How Do You Spell Channukkahh." Tom Lehrer, famous as a kind of musical comedian, came out with "(I'm Spending) Hanukkah in Santa Monica."

Just as Jews contributed mightily to Christmas music, Gentiles have created inspired Chanukah songs. Rapper Too $hort recorded "Hanukkah Song (Favorite Time of the Year)." *Sharon Jones & the Dap-Kings* have a blues-inflected "8 Days of Hanukkah." Mormon Orrin Hatch, together with Jewish Madeline Stone, wrote a song also entitled "8 Days of Hanukkah." Although the latter two songs have identical titles, they are different songs. The *Sharon Jones & the Dap-Kings* song begins, "One, two, three, four, five, six, seven, eight/Days of love/Days of eight/Days of Hanukkah." The Hatch-Stone creation starts, "Hanukkah, oh Hanukkah/The festival of light/In Jerusalem/The oil burned bright." The legendary Woody Guthrie was undoubtedly influenced by his second marriage to a Jewish lady in authoring such songs as "Happy Joyous Hanukkah" and "Hanukkah Dance."

The number of motion pictures with a Chanukah theme does not rival the number of Christmas films. Indeed, this author only found a handful of movies centered around Judaism's December holiday. The most controversial is a comedy/fantasy/action film entitled *The Hebrew Hammer* (2003) that was written and directed by Jonathan Kesselman. The title is the nickname of Mordechai Jefferson Carver (Adam Goldberg) who must save Chanukah from Damian Claus (Andy Dick), the son of Santa Claus. Damian Claus is not tolerant of other holidays but aims to eliminate both Chanukah and Kwanzaa so Christmas will have December all to itself. There are, of course, odd echoes of both *The Grinch Who Stole Christmas* and *The Nightmare Before Christmas* in this bizarre storyline. The motion picture carries deliberate echoes of the "blaxploitation" films that became so popular in the 1970s. That inspiration and parallel is underlined by the fact that Melvin Van Peebles, whose *Sweet Sweetback's Badasssss Song* made blaxploitation history, has a cameo in the film and his son, Mario Van Peebles, plays Mohammed of the Kwanzaa Liberation Front, who joins forces with the "Hammer." JTA writes that the hero "has become a go-to symbol of Jewish toughness" with his "yarmulke and a necklace with a machine gun pendant." Goldberg has said that the movie is about "owning Jewish stereotypes and subverting them." The movie features an organization called the "Jewish Justice League" that is a kind of take-off on the Anti-Defamation League. JTA writes, "Multiple Jewish groups, notably the Anti-Defamation League, were upset" by *The Hebrew Hammer* because they believed it was "perpetuating stereotypes." Writing for *Salon*, Baz Dreisinger interviewed Kesselman about the movie. Dreisinger reports, "Kesselman recalls that at the Berlin screening, an 'older Israeli consulate member walked out.'" However, there are many Jews who like the film.

Two popular Chanukah-themed films are animated. One is the 1986 *An American Tail*. Targeted principally at a child audience — its very title is a wry play on words — the story of *An American Tail* begins in 1885 Czarist Russia. A family of mice named the Mousekewitzes are happily celebrating Chanukah. The Mousekewitzes reside with a human family named Moskowitz who are also Chanukah celebrants. Oops! The festivities of both families are interrupted when a bunch of Cossacks attack the Moskowitz family — and Cossack cats attack the Mousekewitzes! Both two-legged and four-legged M families see their homes destroyed. But all is not lost: the Mousekewitzes board a steamer headed to America — and a variety of incidents ensue that beautifully echo the tribulations and triumphs of similarly situated Jews who fled persecution for the land of liberty.

The other Chanukah-themed animated motion picture, released in 2002, is *Eight Crazy Nights*. This flick was the cinematic launching pad for Sandler's "The Hanukkah Song." *Eight Crazy Nights* centers around a Jewish character named Davey Stone who is known in his fictional town of Dukesberry, New Hampshire as a no-goodnick with a long rap sheet and a great liking for liquor. A series of trials both literal and figurative lead to a kind of moral redemption that is symbolized by an attempt to rescue a Chanukah card that belonged to his dead parents from a trailer that is burning down. Davey hearkens back to the original miracle that led to the creation of Chanukah and his character is rehabilitated through his emotional connection with the Chanukah story. *Eight Crazy Nights* did not make money on its release nor did it get many positive reviews. However, in the years since its release, *Eight Crazy Nights* has attained a kind of cult film status among some Jews.

In 2003, the Disney Channel aired *Full-Court Miracle*, a film revolving around Chanukah. Based on a true story, the movie begins with a group of young Jewish basketball players during Chanukah season looking for a coach good enough to lift them out of a slump. They think of their quest as a search for a kind of Judah Maccabee of the basketball court!

Chanukah has long been cherished by Jews and is typically celebrated with a sense of fun. However, Rabbi Greenberg seems on solid ground when he insists that the true meaning of this holiday is serious. It originated with the battle to save Judaism as a "particularist" faith. Throughout history, the rabbi argues, "Jews have continued to force the world — down to this day — to accept the limits of centralization." There have been a multitude of belief systems that advocate a "universalism that denies the rights of the particular to exist." This Jewish authority asserts, "Universalism must surrender its overweening demands and accept the universalism of pluralism. Only when the world admits that oneness comes out of particular existences, linked through overarching unities, will it escape the inner dynamics of conformity that lead to repression and cruelty." Chanukah exists and is celebrated because Jews throughout history have so strongly insisted on their right to be Jewish.

Chapter 6
Kwanzaa, Yule/Winter Solstice, and Other Special December Days

It should be noted that, although Christmas is a beautiful holiday celebrated by many non-Christians and especially treasured by Christians, there are Christians who do not celebrate Christmas. Often the pagan roots of the holiday are the reason they shun this holiday. As already noted, the Puritans of the past declared an actual "War on Christmas." There are Christians of the present who do not do Christmas. The Jehovah's Witnesses are one example of a well-known Christian denomination that does not regard Christmas as a holiday. There are others including some members of the Religious Society of Friends, commonly called Quakers, and the Churches of Christ denomination. According to Chris Pifer, a spokesperson for a Quaker organization called the Friends General Conference, many Friends eschew Christmas because they believe "every day is a holy day" while others observe the holiday. Church of Christ pastor Ralph Gilmore told a journalist that "the majority of the group's 26,000 congregations do not emphasize Christmas" but acknowledged that individual members might celebrate it "as a matter of private faith" and some Church of Christ "congregations will have a tree at the front of the sanctuary." Gilmore continued that, as a church pastor, "I would often talk about the birth of Jesus because people had it on their minds but most of us would not recognize it as a God-authorized holiday."

What's more, Christmas and Chanukah are not the only major holidays in December. There are other special days of both contemporary and ancient origin.

Kwanzaa: The Twentieth Century Creation of a Cultural Holiday

Kwanzaa is a secular holiday of modern creation that celebrates the rich cultural heritages of black Americans as well as Africans and people of the African Diaspora. Dr. Maulana Karenga, a well-known activist in the Black Power movement of the 1960s and '70s, born Ronald Everett and known for some of his life as Ron Karenga, founded this festival in 1966 to give Americans of black African descent a special time to honor their own culture. It starts on December 26, the day after Christmas, and lasts through New Year's Day of January 1. Karenga took the name "Kwanzaa" from a Swahili word meaning "first fruits." It lasts seven days.

The Nguzo Saba, or Seven Principles, of Kwanzaa, which Karenga expressed in Swahili, are Umoja (unity), Kujichagulia (self-determination), Ujima (collective work and responsibility), Ujamaa (cooperative economics), Nia (purpose), Kuumba (creativity), and Imani (faith). Kwanzaa also has Seven Symbols — also expressed in Swahili. They are maze (nuts, fruits, vegetables), meek (place mat), kinara (candleholder), vibunzi (ear of corn), zawadi (gifts), kikombe cha umoja (communal cup of unity), and mishumbaa saba (seven candles).

The new holiday of Kwanzaa resembles the old holiday of Chanukah in featuring a special candle holder and making candle lighting a central part of its rituals. The kinara has seven candles with a black candle in the middle, three red ones to its left and three green ones to its right. On each day of Kwanzaa, those celebrating it — usually family and/or friends — join to light one of the candles and to discuss the principle for that day. On December 31, Kwanzaa celebrants have a feast called a "karamu."

Seven Principles, Seven Symbols, seven candles in the kinara, all for a festival lasting seven days. Dorothy Winbush Riley observes in *The Complete Kwanzaa: Celebrating Our Cultural Harvest*, "The number seven has always been considered sacred." Thus, the earth was said to be created in six days with the Creator resting on the seventh. Weeks are made of seven days.

The kinara's middle black candle represents Umoja, or Unity, while the green candles to the right symbolize Kujichagulia (self-determination), Ujima (collective work and responsibility), Ujamaa (cooperative economics) and the red candles to the left are emblematic of Nia (purpose), Kuumba (creativity), and Imani (faith). "During Kwanzaa, one candle, representing one principle, is lit each day," Riley explains. "Then the other candles are relit to give off more light and vision." The colors black, red, and green come from the pan-African flag created by pan-Africanist Marcus Garvey. "The kinara is the center of the Kwanzaa setting and represents the original stalk from which we came: our ancestry. The kinara can be any shape — straight lines, semicircles, or spirals — as long as the seven candles are separate and distinct, like a candelabra."

In founding Kwanzaa, Karenga took inspiration from traditional African customs. Thus, the kikombe cha umoja (communal cup of unity) that is used in the libation during the sixth Kwanzaa day at the Karamu feast resembles the practice among some African societies of pouring libations for the dead. "During the Karamu feast, the kikombe cha umoja is passed to family members and guests, who drink from it to promote unity," Riley states. "Then the eldest person present pours the libation (tambiko), usually water, juice, or wine, in the direction of the four winds — north, south, east, and west — to honor the ancestors."

On each of the seven days of the festival, celebrants are expected to greet each other with "Habari gani," which means "What's happening?" The response should be the principle of the day, i.e., "Umoja!" on the first day, "Kujichagulia" on the second, and so on until January 1 when "Imani" is the response.

Riley included a "sample program" for Kwanzaa observance in her book.

She wrote that a typical Kwanzaa day celebration begins with an opening statement, usually by the host or the oldest individual present, followed by a libation to the ancestors, a statement about that day's principle, the lighting of the candles, and ending with a cultural expression that could take the form of the revising of a poem, the playing of music, or something similar. Historical events may be discussed and a final statement may bring the Kwanzaa observance to a close. The final, seventh day of Kwanzaa features a feast and gift giving. Gifts are given and received on the seventh and last day of Kwanzaa. "Handmade gifts are encouraged to promote self-determination, purpose, and creativity and to avoid the chaos of shopping and conspicuous consumption during the December holiday season," Riley comments. In *Kwanzaa: From Holiday to Every Day*, Maitefa Angaza writes similarly of how gifts crafted by the giver are appropriate Kwanzaa gifts: "The exchanging of zawadi [Kwanzaa gifts], when done in the spirit of Kwanzaa, should be stress-free and enriching for both giver and the receiver. The focus is never on trends, price tags, or appearances, so feel free to show your appreciation for others in a creative and affordable manner."

In 2009, a study found that 1-5% of African-Americans, that is, between 500 thousand and two million people, celebrate Kwanzaa. In 2015, a survey by the National Retail Federation found that roughly six million people in the United States celebrate Kwanzaa. It is also celebrated outside America. Angaza observed in her book, which was published in 2007, that Kwanzaa "remains vibrant and growing in relevance. Throughout North America and in areas of South America, the Caribbean, Africa, and Europe, it's won devoted adherents. In fact, it is said that more than 20 million people across the world now gather with family and friends to light the candles, sing the songs, and dedicate themselves to the life-affirming values at Kwanzaa's core."

It should be noted that black Americans who celebrate Kwanzaa often celebrate Christmas as well -- and that the vast majority of Americans of African ancestry celebrate Christmas. In addition, Kwanzaa can be celebrated by people who are not of African descent. Writer Kendall Trammell states, "Clearly it's a holiday created for African-Americans. But just like people other than Mexicans celebrate Cinco de Mayo, other races and ethnic groups are welcome to participate in the Kwanzaa rituals." Another writer, Akilah Bolden-Monifa, notes that "cultural sensitivity is appropriate" since "a big part of the holiday is creating community among African-Americans." Bolden-Monifa elaborates, "When invited, I go to cultural and religious celebrations that are not part of my cultural or religious heritage. I participate in a way that is comfortable for my host and for me. It would be arrogant of me, a non-Jew, to dominate a Seder or Hanukkah celebration, for example. People who are not of African descent should approach Kwanzaa with the same attitude."

The vitality of Kwanzaa has been recognized by major businesses as well as top political leaders. The first Kwanzaa Hallmark card was issued in 1992. Hallmark has continued to issue Kwanzaa cards and many other companies also issue Kwanzaa cards. The United States Post Office issued its first Kwanzaa stamp in 1997. The website of the US Postal Service relates, "New designs were also issued in 2004, 2009, 2011, 2013, and 2016." It has also issued a "Forever" stamp honoring this holiday. A Forever stamp is one that will always equal the current First Class Mail one-ounce price. The Forever stamp carries an image of Floyd Cooper's art depicting a man, woman, and child of African ancestry wearing mixed Western and African clothing. The three, apparently a family, are gathered before a table covered with such standard Kwanzaa items as the straw mat, the kinara with its seven candles, fruits and vegetables, and a unity cup. In 1997, the year the US Post Office issued the first Kwanzaa stamp, President Bill Clinton made the first presidential declaration about Kwanzaa. In 2019, President Donald Trump sent "season's greetings to those observing Kwanzaa both in the United States and around the world."

The Black Candle, a documentary about Kwanzaa, was released in November 2008. The multi-talented and highly esteemed writer Maya Angelou narrated the film that was directed by M. K. Asante. The Africa World Documentary Film Festival 2009 gave *The Black Candle* its award for Best Full-Length Documentary.

Kwanzaa is also the subject of controversy. That controversy is, to some extent, due to the tumultuous life history of its founder.

Born Ron Everett in Parsonburg, Maryland, he moved to California in 1958. In the Sunshine State, he attended Los Angeles City College (LACC) and UCLA. At LACC, he was active in campus activities and enjoyed the distinction of being the first black elected Student Body President. He soon became active in the burgeoning Civil Rights and Black Power movements, joining the Congress of Racial Equality (CORE) and the Student Nonviolent Coordinating Committee (SNCC). At UCLA, he earned a Bachelor's cum laude in 1963 in Political Science with an African Studies specialization. In 1964, he received a Master's in the same subject areas. It was while a college student that he changed his name to Karenga, a Swahili word for "keeper of tradition" and "Maulenga," the latter a word in both Swahili and Arabic meaning "master teacher."

He quit work on a doctorate to devote more time to African American causes. Together with Hakim Jamal, a cousin of Malcolm X, and others, he helped found *US* magazine — the "US" being "us black people." Then they founded an organization called US. In interviews, Karenga cited Malcolm X as a major influence on his own thinking, particularly "nationalism and Pan-Africanism."

A rivalry came about between US and the Black Panthers. To make matters much worse, the FBI deliberately exacerbated tensions between the organizations by sending forged letters to each group pretending to be from the other group. This government-encouraged rivalry led to violence between US and the Black Panthers that resulted in injuries and even deaths. There are unproven reports that Karenga accepted financial and other support from the government for anti-Panther actions.

In 1971, several years after Karenga created Kwanzaa, he was convicted of felonious assault and false imprisonment. He was sentenced to one to ten years in prison. The crimes described in court were genuine atrocities. The victims were two women, Deborah Jones and Gail Davis, previously involved with US. One of them testified that Karenga, together with accomplices including his wife, stripped her of her clothing and beat her with an electrical cord. Karenga's wife, Brenda Karenga, was estranged from him at the time of the trial. She testified that she had sat on the other victim while a man forced water into her mouth through a hose. Jones testified that a hot soldering iron was forced into Davis's mouth and shoved against her face. She also testified that Karenga himself put detergent and running hoses in the mouths of both victims.

The motive for such violence? According to the testimony of both Jones and Brenda Karenga, Karenga believed the two women who were attacked had been conspiring to poison him.

Karenga denied the charges and accused the prosecution of being politically motivated. However, he was convicted. In Karenga's absence, US lost direction and was disbanded in 1975. Karenga was paroled in 1975. In the many years since, he has refused to discuss the crimes and (understandably) omits them from the biographical materials he puts out about himself.

Upon his parole, he put together a new US organization. He also earned a Ph.D. for a dissertation on African American nationalism. As of this writing, he is chair of the Africana Studies Department at California State University, Long Beach. He has published several books, one of which, *Introduction to Black Studies,* is a textbook.

Although Karenga has accomplished much throughout his life, there is no question that his story has some aspects that are morally repulsive. The wrongs he was convicted of doing — and some he is only alleged to have done — combine to provide fodder for an occasional column decrying Kwanzaa by conservative columnist Ann Coulter. On December 27, 2017, Coulter ran a column entitled, "Happy Kwanzaa! The Holiday Brought To You By The FBI." Two years later, she re-ran this same anti-Kwanzaa column. The column begins by stating that Kwanzaa is "celebrated exclusively by white liberals" and calls it a "fake holiday" that was "invented by black radical/FBI stooge Ron Karenga — aka Dr. Maulana Karenga." The latter is a reference to unproven accusations that Karenga has been an FBI informant.

However, it must be asked: Does the fact that the founder of something may have committed a horrible crime mean that he or she could not also have done something that is good? It would be difficult to find a public person who has not done things that are questionable or even awful. This author does not believe that Kwanzaa must be rejected because of the possible crimes of its founder. What's more, Coulter is sarcastic to the point of being just plain wrong when she asserts that Kwanzaa is "celebrated exclusively by white liberals." It continues to be celebrated by a great number of black people decades after its founding because it speaks powerfully to many people of African descent.

The Modern Pagan Revival of the Celebration of Yule/Winter Solstice

The modern era has seen much ferment in religious beliefs as it has in social and political beliefs. There has been a resurgence in people practicing various forms of paganism. These modern faiths are described as "neopaganism," "modern Paganism," and "contemporary Paganism" and are quite varied. There is dispute as to what term to use with some disliking the term "neopaganism." Many authorities in the area call polytheistic believers in the last few centuries "modern Pagans" and those of the distant past "pagans," capitalizing the "P" for the former group but not the latter.

Modern Pagan faiths are polytheistic in form but the adherents of these religions differ in how they interpret the gods, goddesses, and other beings with some believing they actually exist as supernatural entities and others viewing them as metaphors. Those who think there are actual supernatural entities are often called "hard" polytheists while those interpreting them metaphorically are referred to as "soft" polytheists. Modern Pagans can have views that are monotheistic, pantheistic, agnostic, or even atheistic, depending on how they view the gods and goddesses. Some have animistic beliefs, attributing a kind of spiritual essence to animals, plants, rocks, bodies of water, wind, and even human-created objects. Animism can also mean believing the entire universe is organized by a kind of spirit. Some contemporary Pagans combine different Pagan belief systems; some even attempt to combine paganism with mainstream Western religions like Christianity or Judaism. Modern

Pagans do not claim their religion is spiritually the "only way" so they do not proselytize and have no missionaries. Despite the absence of proselytizing, modern Paganism has enjoyed a vibrant growth in recent decades as many people find that polytheistic beliefs "speak" powerfully to them.

In the United States, the most popular contemporary Pagan faiths are, in order of popularity, Wicca, Druidry, and Asatru.

It is important to immediately point out that Wiccans, who not infrequently refer to themselves and their fellows as "witches," and who typically describe organized Wiccan groups as "covens," are not Satanists or devil worshippers. Indeed, Wiccans are themselves quick to make this distinction and disclaim any relationship with "Satanic" beliefs. They point out that Satan is a Christian entity, not even a being recognized as existing in Wicca. Those who practice Wicca are divided as to whether or not it is a revival of an ancient belief system. There are Wiccans who see it as a pre-Christian, nature-based religion that was suppressed for many centuries but has enjoyed a rebirth in modern times. There are others who see it as essentially a faith that originated in modern times. Another point is that some Wiccans embrace the term "witch" while others do not and some who call themselves witches are not part of Wicca. The *Encyclopedia Britannica* states, "Although there were precursors to the movement, the origin of modern Wicca can be traced to a retired British civil servant, Gerald Brousseau Gardner (1884-1964)." Gardner had spent much time in Asia where he took a special interest in occult beliefs and practices. He also read widely in Western literature related to occult topics. The religious movement he founded is, the *Encyclopedia Britannica* explains, "based on a reverence of nature, the practice of magic, and the worship of a female deity (the Goddess) and numerous associated deities (such as the Horned God)." Soon after Gardner popularized his ideas, other Wiccan movements or "traditions" — a word used in the sense of "denomination" in Christianity — emerged. One is Alexandrian Wicca, described by The Celtic Connection website as "very close to Gardnerian" and having rituals that are "very formal." Another is Dianic Wicca, which concentrates on the Goddess. The Celtic Connection discusses two major

Dianic Wicca branches, one of which "gives primacy to the Goddess in its theology, but honors the Horned God as Her Beloved Consort" and has mixed-gender covens. The other branch, "focuses exclusively on the Goddess and consists of women-only covens and groups." Most Wiccan groups base their morality on the "Wiccan Rede" that declares, "As Ye Harm None, Do What Ye Will." This could easily be misinterpreted as no morality at all but "As Ye Harm None" applies to oneself, other human beings, and, according to The Celtic Connection, means "living in harmony with all things that exist" including "the earth, trees, rivers, lakes, oceans, air, and all of earth's creatures."

Although, as noted, Wicca has no relationship to Satanism, there is often prejudice against Wiccans. As the Religious Tolerance website observes, "References to Pagans and Paganism in the Christian Bible are universally negative." Partly because of this, many of today's Pagans do not reveal their beliefs to people around them. Pagans who are open about their faith — whether Wicca or not — are sometimes whimsically said to be "out of the broom closet." The Religious Tolerance website also observes, "As more Neopagans have come out of the [broom] closet and gone public with their faith, more non-pagans have realized the benign nature of Neopagan religious traditions." At least some Wiccans have enjoyed a certain amount of "Establishment" recognition. History.com observes that one prominent Wiccan, Laurie Cabot, "began to gain attention in the United States in the late 1960s teaching classes at Salem State College" and was known for her occult bookstore and her founding of the "Witches' Ball." In 1977, Massachusetts Governor Michael Dukakis declared Cabot the "Official Witch of Salem." Getting recognition by a state governor is definitely getting mainstream! A more recent example of the mainstreaming of modern Paganism is what has been called the "Veteran Pentacle Quest." After a decade of litigation, the US Department of Veterans Affairs (VA) added the pentacle – a Wiccan symbol – to the list of belief emblems that can be places on the grave markers of America's military veterans. In an article on the Veteran Pentacle Quest, prominent Wiccan priestess Rev. Selena Fox wrote, "The

Veteran Pentacle Quest victory is an important breakthrough for equal rights on behalf of Wiccans, Pagans, and other practitioners of Nature religion."

The second most common contemporary Pagan strain in America is that of Druidism. As the name suggests, this group hearkens back to the beliefs and practices of pre-Christian peoples, particularly Celtic, on the British Isles. "Group" rather than "Faith" was used because modern people who consider themselves Druids are heavily divided as to whether or not they are following a faith. Some contemporary Druids regard themselves as participating in a cultural interest/hobby group or subscribing to a philosophical system. Others do indeed regard their Druidry as a faith. Historians often dispute any link between modern and ancient Druidry. The Human Truth Foundation reports, "The most common refrain from historians is that so little is known about Celtic Druidry that is not possible to draw sensible inferences." The same website continues, "Some Druids are pagan, some are Christians (which went through a phase of trying to convince everyone that Druidry was a monotheistic precursor to Christianity) and some Druids are completely secular and merely enjoy cultural artifacts." A religious group called A Druid Fellowship describes itself as "part of the larger NeoPagan movement" and elaborates that "we are polytheistic nature worshippers." *Bishop's Encyclopedia of Religions, Society and Philosophy* states, "Many Neo-Druids are pantheists who view God as being present within and connected to the natural world" and have "a passionate reverence for nature, the Earth, and the body." A fusion of pantheism and polytheism is evident in many modern Pagan faiths and the website of a Druid religious group called Ár nDraíocht Féin (ADF) states, "we believe that divinity is intrinsically present in the material and natural world, including in human nature. Divinity manifests as an uncountable number of beings, commonly called the Gods and Spirits." The ADF also states, "We believe that divinity is as likely to manifest in a female form as it is in a male form, and that the word 'Goddesses' makes just as much sense as 'Gods'" since "women and men are spiritually equal." Druids typically believe in an "Otherworld" to which souls travel upon death but also believe it can be visited during this life time through such means as meditation and trances.

Meditation, like prayer, is central to contemporary Druidism. Today's Druids usually describe their organized groups as "groves," a term that is especially appropriate since the faith emphasizes a sacred aspect to trees and religious meetings often take place outdoors. In a section on Neo-Druid ethics and morality, the ADF states that these things "should be based on joy, love, self-esteem, mutual respect, the avoidance of harm to ourselves and others, and the increase of public benefit."

Third on the list of modern Pagan groups in America are those who follow ancient Norse/Germanic beliefs. This neopagan denomination is called by various names with Asatru, Heathenism, and Odinism among the most prominent. The Religion Facts website relates, "Ancient Norse paganism and modern Asatru are polytheistic," having primary gods and goddesses as well as "minor deities and other supernatural beings of varying importance." Practitioners of this faith are divided as to whether or not the deities exist as actual spiritual entities or should be understood as metaphors. Ethics in this religion tend to consist of trying to adhere to the "Nine Noble Virtues," usually seen as courage, truth, honor, fidelity, discipline, hospitality, industriousness, self-reliance, and perseverance. Asatru groups often call themselves kindreds. A major ritual is that of the "blot" which is typically the offering of mead, beer, or cider to gods and/or goddesses. Religion Facts states, "The liquid is consecrated to a god or goddess, then the worshippers drink a portion of it and pour the rest as a libation."

Followers of Germanic/Norse beliefs are severely split among themselves on their beliefs about race and racism. The "folkish" believe that only those of European ancestry can be part of the faith; the "universalist" believe the faith open to people of all ethnicities and races. Steve McNallen, founder of the Asatru Folk Assembly (AFA), writes that Asatru is "a religion not for all of humanity, but rather one that calls only its own." McNallen believes it is a faith for white people only. Although McNallen's sentiments are clearly racist, he says that he does not dislike anyone on the basis of his or her race, does not believe any race superior to another, and is a white "separatist" rather than "supremacist." Indeed, the Southern Poverty Law Center (SPLC) observes that McNallen has been criticized by more extreme folkish believers "as a race traitor" because he does not "consistently support white supremacy."

It is important to recognize that many, probably most, who practice Norse Paganism are "universalist" and strongly reject racism. The SPLC states that "no form of paganism is inherently bigoted." One Asatru organization, The Troth, is adamant in its universalism, stating on its website: "Membership in the Troth and participation in our activities is open to worthy folks regardless of race, ethnic origin, gender or sexual orientation, and we do not permit discrimination on these grounds in the activities of the Troth or any of its affiliated groups."

Just as Asatru followers differ greatly in their views on race, they also differ in their views on gender. As the SPLC reports, Folkish Asatru tends to promote "rigid gender roles," seeing women "as keepers of the home and bearers of life." Universalist Asatru is more apt to oppose gender discrimination, promoting equal attention to female and male deities as well as not discriminating on the basis of gender regarding its clergy.

Gender is highlighted in the entire modern Pagan movement as a large branch of it focuses on Goddess worship. This group tends to have strong feminist concerns. Molly Hanson, a journalist who often writes about religious and occult subjects, speculates that the "rejection of institutionalized, patriarchal religions might account for the specific cultural interest in the Wiccan branch of neopaganism." Hanson continues that prominent Wiccan priestess Starhawk asserts that "reclaiming the word 'witch' is to reclaim a woman's right to be powerful and to celebrate aspects of the divine that have been traditionally associated with 'the feminine.'" It should be mentioned that there are Goddess worshippers who are male. Some Goddess worshippers believe in an actual female higher power, or multiple female supernatural deities, some believe that the earth is itself a goddess they often call "Gaia," and some see the Goddess as a metaphor for female powers and empowerment.

Although Wicca, Druidry, and Asatru are probably the largest neopagan groups in the United States, there are also contemporary Pagans who follow ancient Greek, Roman, Egyptian, Semitic, African, indigenous American, and other belief systems. Additionally, and as previously noted, many modern Pagans combine and/or synthesize multiple belief systems. Contemporary Pagan John Halstead observes that there are many contemporary Pagans, often called "eclectic Pagans," who do not follow any particular recognized "path" in contrast to those who adhere to "more traditional or retrospective" belief systems. Dennis Carpenter, an author known for his scholarly articles on Paganism and husband of Selena Fox, has described Paganism in the last few centuries as a "synthesis of historical inspiration and present-day creativity." Halstead also remarks that contemporary Pagans "may worship or honor one or more gods from ancient myth or even modern gods of their own imaginations."

Molly Hanson observes, "The central underpinning belief that unifies the varied groups is a deep reverence for nature. Often, neopagans adhere to animistic beliefs" including the idea that all objects, whether animate or inanimate, are "imbued with a living soul." She elaborates, "Consistent with the view that all of the natural world is alive, neopagans revere the earth as a living being." They tend to believe in the "immanence of a divine presence that both permeates the natural world and transcends it."

What is the draw of modern Paganism? "Neo-paganism might well be a reaction against what Max Weber referred to as the 'disenchantment of the world' whereby modern life and scientific advancement have drained a sense of the sacred from our lives," Hanson speculates. For anyone unfamiliar with Max Weber (1864-1920), he was a German sociologist and philosopher who strongly influenced social theories, and wrote important essays about the sociology of religion. Halstead expresses similar sentiments when he writes, "Neo-Pagans feel that human beings have become tragically disconnected from the natural world and our natural selves" so they "seek to heal this rift by reconnecting with the sacred dimension of nature. This is sometimes referred to as 're-enchanting the world.'"

The holiday most strongly associated with modern Paganism is Samhain that falls on October 31st. They observe this as an especially sacred day at the same time their neighbors celebrate the whimsical trick-or-treating holiday of Halloween. Halstead notes, "Due to the coincidence of these two holidays, as well as contemporary Paganism's association with Witchcraft, this is the time of the year when Pagans tend to get the most media coverage."

Many of today's Pagans also have a special holiday in December. For people following revived pagan faiths, the revered December holiday is apt to fall on December 21 or close to it, but it is the Winter Solstice or Yule rather than Christmas. An interesting part of Pagan Yule celebration is that such observances have much in common with Christmas celebration since, as Selena Fox notes in "13 Ways to Celebrate Yuletide" on the website Circle Sanctuary – and has been previously explored in this book -- "Christmas Eve and Christmas, New Year's Eve and New Year's Day have their origins in Winter Solstice celebrations of a variety of Pagan cultures through the ages." Fox writes that plants such as "evergreen wreaths & boughs, mistletoe, holly" are as appropriate for Yule as for Christmas. She advises contemporary Pagans to "harvest a Yule tree," set it up in the home, and "decorate it with lights" and "sun symbols." Fox continues that, just as the majority of the public relishes Christmas songs, her sister and brother neopagans can "Listen to Pagan Yuletide music" and may wish to "create a Yuletide chant, poem, or song." She suggests burning a "Yule Log" and meditating on the rising and/or "setting of the Solstice Sun." Pagans should not imitate the pre-reform Ebenezer Scrooge, Fox indicates, but should "contribute to a charity" to "spread the joy of Yuletide." Fox urges that modern Pagans, "focus on world peace and planetary well-being" in their "rituals, meditations, prayers, and other workings."

Ceisiwr Serith is an author and a member of the Druid fellowship called Ár nDraíocht Féin. He is also a teacher of contemporary Paganism who has worked extensively with both Wiccan covens and Druid groves. His book, *A Book of Pagan Prayer*, contains three prayers specifically for Yule. One untitled prayer begins: "This is the long night/This is the dark night/This is the cold night/This is the night of last hope." It continues that this is the night of "the little spark" and the "turning from darkness" as the "turning toward light." It ends with "call all beings to warm themselves at our fires." The prayer repeatedly emphasizes the specialness of the night and how that specialness grows from nature. Thus, the prayer speaks powerfully to the reverence for nature that is intrinsic to much of neopaganism. It also proclaims that Yule is a special turning point, a signal to embrace hope, to nurture the "little spark" of that hope in turning from darkness toward light and wonder. Serith also has a prayer for Yule entitled "The Goddess" and another entitled "Sun." Part of "The Goddess" comments, "Even in the cold time, when everything seems dead, each moment is born after its predecessor and time goes on: you give birth even in the poverty of winter." In "The Sun," part of Serith's prayer says, "I pray to you, new sun, Reborn, O Lord, from the dark."

On the "Paganism and Wicca" section of the Learn Religions website, Patti Wigington has a chapter called "All About Yule" in which she notes, "For people of nearly any religious background, the time of the winter solstice is a time when we gather with family and loved ones. For Pagans and Wiccans, it's often celebrated as Yule, but there are literally dozens of ways you can enjoy the season." Among the "rituals and ceremonies" are the setting up of a Yule altar, specific Yule prayers, a "Yule log ceremony," and a "Yule Cleansing Ritual." She talks about how Pagans and Wiccans often celebrate Yule with family and friends. She discusses a "Winter Solstice Party." Some in this group engage in practices quite similar to those of their Christmas celebrating neighbors such as exchanging gifts and "holiday trees." Wigington continues that pagans and Wiccans are unlikely to decorate their trees with "a little baby Jesus or a bunch of crosses" but may well hang them with "suns and solar ornaments," "pipe cleaner pentacles," "natural objects like acorns, feathers, holly, mistletoe or pine cones," and "magical items" such as "cups, wands, or daggers."

An essay entitled "10 Ways To Celebrate Yule Without A Coven" appears on a website called Tetraktys. The title of the website is a word for a triangular figure made up of ten points in four rows, a figure that was considered a mystic symbol in Ancient Greece by Pythagoreans. The author of the article, Tsona, opens, "Hello witches! If you didn't know already, Yule is the pagan and Wiccan celebration of the winter solstice." Like Selena Fox, Tsona reminds readers that "a lot of Christmas traditions have pagan roots" which means "it's very easy to celebrate the winter solstice and the holidays from a pagan point of view." Tsona advises setting up a Yule tree and a Yule altar, observing that there are no "strict rules" for a Yule altar but today's Pagans often customize them according to their specific beliefs and wishes. Tsona continues, "Making your own pagan ornaments is a great activity to do by yourself or with your family!" Other Yule activities could include getting a tarot reading, burning a Yule Log, creating a "Yule Incense Blend," creating Yule candles, and reading Yule stories. Toward the article's end, Tsona declares, "Yule is one of my favorite holidays (with Samhain, of course!)."

The Druid Network website relates that modern Druids celebrate a "festival of Midwinter" and continues that "although Druids don't celebrate Christmas, the winter rites are held on and around the same days. Midwinter in the Druid tradition is called Alban/Arthan, Welsh/Brythonic for 'the light of the bear.'" The reason for this title? "For some it is understood to imply both the constellation of the Great Bear in our northern winter skies, and also Arthur, the savior king and mythic hero of the British Isles."

In the United Kingdom, contemporary Druids, along with many others, flock to Stonehenge around Yule. A 2018 *BBC* article by Sophie Wilkinson reported on Druids who were celebrating "the winter solstice" on December 21 "at an ancient monument at Hilsea Lines near Portsmouth." Druid Priestess Laura Brown related that the "Druidic Oath" would be chanted. "We repeat it three times," she stated. "'We swear by peace and love to stand heart to heart and hand in hand, mark us spirit, hear us now confirming this, our sacred vow and we will chant." Following this, Druids would read aloud poetry inspired by Celtic myths and/or sing songs similarly inspired. The article reported that there would also be an "annual challenge between the Oak King and Holly King" in which two masked Druids would stage a mock battle. Wilkinson writes, "For some people, Christmas begins with a bottle of fizz, but for many Druids, mead, an alcoholic drink made from fermented honey and water, is the tipple of choice." A Druid pointed out that "to make the ceremony inclusive" a non-alcoholic beverage its typically available. A website called The Druid Way points out that Druid Yule celebrations are similar to Christmas since such traditions as "Yule log" are of pagan origin. The Druid Way asserts, "In this darkest time of the year we celebrate the return of the Divine Child, the Mabon, the rebirth of the golden solstice Sun, who will bring warmth, light and life back to Earth again" as "the Sun dies and is reborn."

The Asatru Community website states, "The commencement of the Yuletide celebration has no set date, but is traditionally 12 days long with the start of the festivities beginning at sunset on the winter solstice. Many in Asatru believe Santa Claus was based on the Norse god called Odin. According to The Asatru Community, "The 12 days of Yule is largely devoted to baking cakes, cookies, and breads and making the unique decorations which beautify every Heathen home at this holiday season. There are, for example, intricate paper cutouts to make and put on the walls; stars, wooden toys, straw Goats and Will Boars to hang on the Yule tree." It further comments, "We decorate an evergreen tree with sun wheels, runes, items of food such as cranberries and popped corn, and bright pretty things." A writer to The Troth website stated that, since so much of Christmas celebration began with pagan practice, "We can celebrate alongside our friends and neighbors, understanding the sacred purpose of what we are all doing already." Another writer to The Troth reported that two groups, one of them a kindred, had a "Yule Ball" in British Columbia, Canada. The writer described it as a "masquerade ball" in which over a hundred costumed revelers "gathered to dance, to play, to revel" as they celebrated Yuletide.

Considering all the above, we need not assume that the beautiful evergreen standing in a home during December is a "Christmas" tree — but we can still be confident the tree represents a cherished celebration.

Ho, Ho, Ho, Hey, Hey, Hey — What About that Boxing Day?

Boxing Day is a special day that falls on December 26, the day after Christmas. It originated in Great Britain and that nation, along with countries that either are now affiliated with Britain or were in the past, are those most likely to observe it.

The reason for its peculiar name is not because anyone "slugs it out" with thick gloves in a boxing ring or elsewhere on the day. Nor is it because boxes that were previously filled with gifts are often scattered around places the day after Christmas. Snopes.com explains, "Its origins are found in a long-ago practice of giving cash or durable goods to those of the lower classes. Gifts among equals were exchanged on or before Christmas Day, but beneficences to those less fortunate were bestowed the day after." There is historical dispute as to particulars concerning Boxing Day's origins. One explanation is that there was a time in which it was common practice for merchants to bestow boxes filled with food to servants and tradespeople the day after Christmas. Another is that Christmas Day afforded a time during which, on large manors, servants and their lords/ladies came together so, on the day after Christmas, the servants were handed boxes filled with practical goods. Still another explanation, according to Snopes.com, is, "Boxes in churches for seasonal donations to the needy were opened on Christmas Day, and the contents distributed by the clergy the following day." The latter explanation finds support in the famous *Diary of Samuel Pepys*, dated Dec. 19, 1663, in which Pepys writes that he "gave something to the boys' box against Christmas."

The United States is not big on Boxing Day but it has received official recognition in the state of Massachusetts. On Dec. 5, 1996, Massachusetts Governor William F. Weld responded positively to the efforts of a coalition of people from Britain who wanted to "transport English tradition to the United States" by officially declaring December 26 as Boxing Day in Massachusetts. He did not, however, make it an employee holiday in the state.

Festivus — the Holiday "for the rest of us" that Spun from *Seinfeld*

Propelled by the popular TV sitcom *Seinfeld*, a whimsical secular holiday entitled "Festivus" has become part of the American cultural landscape. Daniel

O'Keefe first celebrated a special day he decided to call "Festivus" in 1966. He chose December 23 as the date for Festivus because it was the anniversary of his first date with a lady named Deborah — who would become his wife. The O'Keefe family tradition of Festivus was written into a *Seinfeld* episode by scriptwriter Dan O'Keefe, son and namesake of Festivus creator.

A *Seinfeld* episode entitled "The Strike" first aired on December 18, 1997. O'Keefe made his family tradition into the family tradition of *Seinfeld* characters Frank and George Constanza. Father Frank created Festivus and son George reacts with embarrassment when reminded that Festivus is part of his familial heritage. Frank informs Cosmo Kramer that Festivus was born out of a Christmas season frustration. Frank was at a department store in a tug-of-war with another Christmas shopper over a doll. "I realized there had to be a better way," Frank recalled of his inspiration for the less-commercial holiday of Festivus. He decided on a new holiday he considered, "A Festivus for the rest of us!"

As was true of the original, the Constanza Festivus is celebrated yearly on December 23. However, unlike O'Keefe practice, the Constanza Festivus boasts a simple aluminum pole in lieu of a Christmas tree. Dan O'Keefe has said the original family Festivus had no pole but boasted a clock inside a bag. Dan O'Keefe does not know the significance of the bagged timepiece.

Like the original, it features a Festivus Dinner, an "Airing of Grievances," and "Feats of Strength."

There is a certain amount of confusion about what constitutes an appropriate "Festivus Dinner." That served on Seinfeld appears to be meatloaf on lettuce but the O'Keefe tradition was usually a turkey or ham. The "Airing of Grievances" has people clearing the air about the year's past disappointments. The "Feat of Strength" is a wrestling match.

From the 1997 *Seinfeld* episode, Festivus has spread. Chicago restaurant publicist Jennifer Galdes organized her first Festivus party in the early 2000s. "More and more people are familiar with what Festivus is and it's growing," she told reporter Allen Salkin in 2004.

Jerry Stiller, the actor who played Frank Constanza, has been called the

Santa Claus of Festivus. "I'll take that mantle," Stiller proclaims. "I'll wear my crown." There is a website specifically devoted to Festivus. *Festivus: The Holiday for the Rest of Us* by Allen Salkin was published by Warner Books in 2010. Jerry Stiller wrote a forward to the book.

Festivus is going strong as of this writing, perhaps because its whimsical character is appealing, perhaps because a holiday based on a sitcom episode is so silly it is also irresistible.

Chapter 7
Happy Holidays . . . to Everyone!

That America's Jews have contributed so much to Christmas says much about the common humanity of Jews and Christians. It also speaks to the ability of people to appreciate the cherished stories and traditions of other people. It does not require belief to see the beauty in the Jesus story. Gentiles can appreciate beauty in Chanukah and other aspects of Judaism. People have appreciated the importance of the winter solstice since time immemorial and the modern Pagans who celebrate Yule/Winter Solstice today draw upon fascinating legends and lore. The modern holiday of Kwanzaa has its critics but it speaks powerfully to many people of African ancestry and should be respected by all of us. The story of Boxing Day is a heartwarming tribute to the virtues of generosity and kindness. The frisky and feisty modern creation called Festivus should bring a smile to anyone possessing that most necessary of coping qualities -- a sense of humor.

Of course, the vast majority of Americans are Christians. Come December, Jewish writers, musicians, actors, and other artists are surrounded by Christmas. Thus, they cannot help but be influenced by this special day to create art — which, of course, in turn influences the celebration of the holiday itself.

In this writer's opinion, there is nothing wrong with wishing someone a "Merry Christmas." Indeed, there is much that is good about it. It is also this author's opinion that there is nothing wrong with saying "Happy Holidays" — and much that is right about it. After all, there are many in this wonderfully diverse land who do not celebrate Christmas. What's more, among the non-Christmas celebrating group are many Christians who reject it as non-Biblical. There are also those who celebrate Chanukah and those who celebrate Yule/Winter Solstice. People of African ancestry who celebrate Kwanzaa are apt to also celebrate Christmas but there are those for whom Kwanzaa is the only major December holiday. Festivus fans, who may or may not also celebrate Christmas, Chanukah, Yule/Winter Solstice, and/or Kwanzaa are out there. "Happy Holidays" is not necessarily better than "Merry Christmas" but it has the advantage of including the other celebrants while by no means ignoring the Christmas loving majority.

Another reason for exclaiming "Happy Holidays" is that New Year's follows Christmas very closely. The slogan puts those two holidays together and expresses a wish that, for the many who celebrate Christmas, the joys of that holiday will carry over into New Year's.

"You can't please everybody" is a truism that might be expanded to "It's hard to include everybody." While New Year's is an inevitable part of everyone's life, there are some people who have no major holiday in December. "Happy Holidays" may be seen as leaving those folks out. It does not follow that it should not be said as it is hard to see it as offensive to anyone.

Getting back to the primary focus of this book, although some people designate Jews the natural enemy of Christmas, the truth is that Jews, often working cooperatively with Gentiles, have enriched beyond measure the celebration of this exquisitely beautiful holiday. This author hopes that *Christmas Gifts from the Chanukah Crowd* will be a modest contribution to increasing our sense of shared humanity.

Bibliography

"8 Days of Hanukkah." Sharon Jones & the Dap-Kings.

"Aaron Russo." Internet Movie Database.

"Aaron Russo on America: From Freedom to Fascism." Gaia.com.

Andrea, Nellie. "'Future Man' Co-Creators Kyle Hunter & Ariel Shaffir Ink Overall Deal With Sony Pictures TV." *Deadline*. April 10, 2019.

"Ariel Shaffir." Internet Movie Database.

Altman, Alex. "A Brief History of the War on Christmas." Time. Dec. 24, 2008.

Angaza, Maitefa. Kwanzaa: From Holiday to Every Day. Kensington Publishing Corp. New York, NY. 2007.

Ankeny, Jason. "Haven Gillespie." Allmusic.

"Asatru." Religion Facts.

Associated Press. "Wal-Mart Opts for 'Christmas' Marketing." NBC News. 11/5/2016.

"A Tale of Santa." The Troth.

Bergreen, Laurence. As Thousands Cheer: The Life of Irving Berlin. Penguin Books USA, Inc. New York, New York. 1990.

Birman, Bryan. "How a Jewish kid from Northeast Philly grew up to create a Christmas classic." *My City Paper*. 12/05/2013.

Bolden-Monifa, Akilah. "Can White People Celebrate Kwanzaa and Other Questions You Were Too Afraid To Ask."SanFrancisco.cbslocal.com. Dec. 24, 2013.

Boston, Rob. "Is There A 'War On Christmas'?" Americans United For Separation of Church and State.

"Christmas." Britannica.com.

Chwast, Seymour. The Miracle of Hanukkah. Blue Apple Books. 2006.

Coulter, Ann. "Happy Kwanzaa! The holiday brought to you by the FBI." mdjonline.com. Dec. 27, 2019.

"Danny Elfman." DannyElfman.com.

"Danny Elfman." Internet Movie Database.

"Danny Kaye Biography." UNICEF

The Diary of Samuel Pepys. Saturday 19 December 1663.

Dixon, Wheeler Winston; Foster, Gwendolyn Audrey. A Short History of Film. Rutgers University Press. New Brunswick, New Jersey. 2008.

Downs, Gordon. "Ari Shaffir on Hollywood Comedy Route, Joe Rogan and Mushrooms." Sandiego.com. June 1, 2011.

Dreisinger, Baz. "The 'Jewsploitation' craze." *Salon*. Dec. 24, 2003.

Drums, Diana. "'Trading Places': More than 7 Things You May Not Know About The Film (But We Won't Bet A Dollar On It). Indiewire. June 8, 2013.

Duke, David. "The Jewish War on Christmas!"

Duke, David. "The European History of Christmas & How a real Ultra-Racist Zio-Grinch Stole It!"

Ebert, Roger. *"Elf."* Nov. 7, 2003. rogerebert.com

Ebert, Roger. *"The Nightmare Before Christmas."* Oct. 22, 1993. rogerebert.com

Ebert, Roger. *"Trading Places."* June 9, 1983. rogerebert.com

Ebert, Roger. *"The Night Before."* rogerebert.com.

"Elf (2003)." Internet Movie Database.

"Elmer Rice." Encyclopedia.com.

"Evan Goldberg." Internet Movie Database.

"A Festivus for the Rest of Us." Lawrence Journal-World.

"Festivus - It's For the Rest of Us!" Holiday Insights.

Film, Gretchen. "St. Nicholas and Your Shoes! A St. Nicholas Tradition." Catholic company.com. Dec. 1, 2016.

Fox, Rev. Selena. "Success in the Veteran Pentacle Quest!" *CIRCLE* Magazine. Fall 2007. Republished on the Circle Sanctuary website.

Greenberg, Rabbi Irving. The Jewish Way: Living the Holidays. Summit Books, Simon & Schuster. New York, New York. 1998.

Halperin, Shirley. "Seth Rogen and Evan Goldberg Launch Canadian Cannabis Company." *Variety*. March 27, 2019.

Halstead, John. "We're Not All Witches: An Introduction to Neo-Paganism." HuffPost.

Hanson, Molly. "Could neopaganism be the new 'religion' of America?" Big Think. Sept. 30, 2019.

Hart, Hugh. "Like A Kid At Christmas." SFGate. Nov. 16, 2003.

"Haven Gillespie." Songhall.

"The Hebrew Hammer." Internet Movie Database.

Himelstein, Rabbi Dr. Shmuel. The Jewish Primer: Questions and Answers on Jewish Faith and Culture. Facts on File. New York/Oxford/Sydney. 1990.

"History of Christmas." History.com.

Jankowski, Paul. "Is Saying 'Merry Christmas' Politically Correct? Who Cares?" Forbes.com. 12/19/2014.

"J. Fred Coots." SongHall.

"John Landis." Freedom From Religion Foundation.

"John Landis." Internet Movie Database.

"Jonathan Levine." *Caviar*.

"Jonathan Levine." Internet Movie Database.

"Joseph Gordon-Levitt." Internet Movie Database.

JTA. "Antisemitic Twitter trolls motivate producers of 'Hebrew Hammer' sequel." *The Jerusalem Post*. Nov. 8, 2017.

Keck, Kristi. "Heated debate again over 'War on Christmas' claims." CNN.com. Dec. 18, 2009.

Kermode, Mark. "The Night Before review — tired Christmas bromance." *The Guardian*. Dec. 6, 2015.

Kimmelman, Leslie. *Write On, Irving Berlin!* Sleeping Bear Press. 2018.

Late, Erin. "Asatru FAQ: How Do I Celebrate Yule?" witchesandpagans.com

Leibovich, Mark. "A Senator's Gift to the Jews, Nonreturnable." *The New York Times*. Dec. 8, 2009.

Linking, Jason. "O'Reilly's War On Christmas Goes Retail." HuffPost. 11/6/2008.

"The Living Theatre." kirkusreviews.com

"Lizzy Caplan." Internet Movie Database.

"Manager Aaron Russo dies at 64." Associated Press. Variety. Aug. 26, 2007.

Mendelson, Scott. Forbes. Oct. 15, 2013.

Merry, Stephanie. "Movie review: Dudes' night out in raunchy-sweet 'The Night Before.'" *The Washington Post*. Nov. 19, 2015.

"Michael Curtiz." Encyclopedia Britannica.

"Modern Druids (Neo-Druidism/Neo-Druidry)." The Human Truth Foundation.

Nashawaty, Chris. Crab Monster, Teenage Cavemen, and Candy Stripe Nurses: Roger Corman: King of the B Movie. Abrams. New York, NY.

"Neopagan & Pagan religious traditions." Religious Tolerance.

"Neo-Volkisch." Southern Poverty Law Center (SPLC).

Ng, David. "Danny Elfman can relate to 'Nightmare Before Christmas' hero Jack Skellington." Los Angeles Times. Oct. 24, 2015.

"*The Night Before*." (2015). Internet Movie Database.

"*The Nightmare Before Christmas*." (1993). Internet Movie Database.

O'Donnell, Jayne. "Wan-Mart wishes you a Merry Christmas." USA Today. 11/8/2205.

O'Malley, JP. "The unknown director behind one of the most famous movies of all time." The Times of Israel. Jan. 14, 2018.

"The Origins of Boxing Day." Snipes.com. Nov. 7, 2000.

Pace, Eric. "Danny Kaye, Limber-Limbed Comedian, Dies." The New York Times. March 4, 1987.

"Paul Reubens." Internet Movie Database.

"Pee-wee Herman is back with a tour, and possibly much more." The Jewish Times. Feb. 4, 2020.

Peterson, Jeffrey. "Telling ghost stories is a lost tradition on Christmas Eve." Deseret News. Dec. 23, 2010.

Pfefferman, Naomi. "A Gift From Santa's Jewish Helpers." Jewish Journal. Dec. 25, 2003.

Popper, Nathaniel. "Boycotts Bloom As Religious Conservatives Wage Battle Over Christmas." Forward.com. Dec. 16, 2005.

Porter, Joel. "Federal judge rules against Concord High School Nativity scene." WNDU.com. Dec. 2, 2015.

Quirk, Lawrence J. James Stewart: Behind The Scenes Of A Wonderful Life. Applause Books. New York. 1997.

Richey, Warren. "Nativity scene is too religious for New York City school." The Christian Science Monitor. Feb. 22, 2007.

Riley, Dorothy Winbush. The Complete Kwanzaa: Celebrating Our Cultural Harvest. HarperCollins Publishers. New York, NY. 1995.

Rodrick, Stephen. "The Liberation of Lizzy Caplan." *Rolling Stone*. Aug. 25, 2015.

Rollins, Samantha. "Lizzy Caplan Has Graduated From Playing 'F*cked-Up Ingenues.'" *Bustle*. Sept. 4, 2019.

Rosenberg, Dan. "The Anti-Semitic Roots of the 'War on Christmas.'" The Canadian Jewish News. April 6, 2020.

Rozsa, Matthew. Dec. 25, 2019.

Ruskin, Karla. A Great Miracle Happened There: A Chanukah Story. Willa Perlman Books. HarperCollins Publishers. New York, NY. 1993.

Sackville, Kerri. "Can Aril Shaffir's jokes about the Holocaust ever be funny?" SBS.com. May 1, 2018.

Salkin, Allen. "Footy to the World: Festivus is Come." The New York Times. Dec. 19, 2004.

"Sears Puts 'Merry Christmas' Signs in its Stores." Newsmax.com. Dec. 7, 2005.

Seraph, Ceisiwr. A Book of Pagan Prayer. Weiser Books. Newburyport, MA. 2018.

"Seth Rogen." Biography.com.

"Seth Rogen." Encyclopedia Britannica.

"Seth Rogen." Internet Movie Database.

Street, Kate. "Do You Know The Story Behind St. Nicholas Day?" Simplemost.com

Strode, Tom. "Target, Sears say they'll include 'Christmas.'" The Ethics and Religious Liberty Commission of The Southern Baptist Convention." 2002.

"Target Includes 'Christmas,' AFA Drops Boycott." Newsmax.com. Dec. 9, 2005.

"Target Merry Christmas Ban." Snopes.com. Dec. 9, 2005.

"Trading Places." Internet Movie Database.

"The Troth."

"The Twilight Zone Case." Denise Noe.

Trammell, Kendall. "A non-black person's guide to Kwanzaa." CNN.com. Dec. 26, 2017.

Wakin, Daniel J. "Lawsuit Attacks Schools' Ban on Nativity Scenes." The New York Times. Dec. 11, 2002.

"Wal-Mart Merry Christmas Ban." Snopes.com.

White, Adam. "Lizzy Caplan: 'After Mean Girls, I didn't work again until I dyed my hair blonde and got a spray tan.'" The Independent. Feb. 13, 2020.

White, Gillian B.; Lam Bourree. "Trading Places: A 1983 Christmas Comedy That's Still Surprisingly Relevant." The Atlantic. Dec. 25, 2015.

"Why is Christmas Day on the 25th December?" whychristmas.com

"What Do Neopagan Druids Believe?" Ár nDraíocht Féin (ADF).

"Who are the Neo-Druids and What do They Believe?" Bishop's Encyclopedia of Religion, Society and Philosophy. Nov. 17, 2019.

"Wicca." The Celtic Connection.

"Wicca." Encyclopedia Britannica.

"Wicca." History.com.

Wilkinson, Sophie. "I'm a young Druid, and this is how I celebrate at Christmastime." BBC.co.uk.

"The Winter Solstice." The Druid Network.

"Winter Solstice — Alban Arthan." The Druid Way.

"Yule." The Asatru Community.

"Yule Ball Courtney BC." The Troth.

www.ingramcontent.com/pod-product-compliance
Lightning Source LLC
Chambersburg PA
CBHW050110170426
43198CB00014B/2519